Carnivore Diet

A High Protein Guide with Delicious Meat Recipes for Metabolism Boost and Muscles Growth Safely

Jason Hollister

TABLE OF CONTENTS

INTRODUCTION

You are welcome to this Amazing Ebook. I am glad to take you through the journey of this book. Taking the Initial step to another healthy lifestyle. You have likely heard the old saying, "your health will depend on the type of food you eat," but as our insight into the human body develops step by step, this maxim rings more authentic than at any other time. What we put inside our bodies is fundamental to our general health – more so than any other factor. This is especially valid in our cutting-edge age when the composition of food has seen drastic changes over the previous century – and not for the better.

How we sustain our bodies isn't just the way to better health but additionally to superior personal satisfaction. A nutritionally poor diet will leave us low on energy, exhausted, and denies us of the chance to become all we can be. Conversely, a diet loaded with great nutritious choices, which includes all the fundamental vitamins and minerals we need, will give us clean energy that won't contaminate our systems and leave us slacking be- rear in life.

As science develops to understand the fundamentals of health more and more, we cannot underestimate the importance of the connection between diet choices and health outcomes. Therefore, we presently appreciate that at the very heart of anything we need to achieve in our lives, great nutrition is essential. Regardless of what your fantasies are, if your body isn't nutritionally balanced, with the perfect measure of minerals, proteins, and vitamins, you will battle to accomplish success in any field.

For years, many purported health specialists have been advocating a switch to a 100 percent plant-based diet, either as a vegan or vegetarian. If this were a natural form of eating, you would imagine that it would be simple for people to accept and incorporate this sort of change in their dietary patterns. However, in a world of right around 8 billion people, it is estimated that, as of the finish of 2018, there were just 1.5 billion who are vegetarians. Of that number, only 75 million are vegetarians by choice. The others are doing so chiefly for strict, family, or societal reasons. It appears people innately realize that meat in the diet is acceptable for them.

These statistics show that paying little mind to what people are stating about the perils of meat (especially red meat), something within us as a species wouldn't like to release it. This is one of the primaries reasons why the carnivore diet is picking up in prominence. It is connecting us back to our traditional developmental roots and, as a rule, was the main diet our ancestors knew and flourished with.

So, the carnivore diet isn't new. It has been around for thousands of tons of years, but here in the following pages, the information you will learn may be different to you – or it might be a few-things you have as of now instinctively comprehended. In any case, this book is planned as a one-stop resource for all that you will ever need to know concerning the carnivore diet, including how to utilize it to your advantage for ideal health, a muscular and athletic body, and fast fat loss.

The following chapters will discuss what the carnivore diet is. We will expound on the outcomes you can expect from the diet and the host of advantages that you will adore. We will include the obstacles you may need to overcome and give a de- followed do's-and-don'ts guide to acing this exciting diet. Also, to top everything off, we have thirty delicious recipes that are simple on the wallet, simple on the stomach and affirmed for the carnivore diet.

Much obliged again for choosing the Carnivore Diet. Each effort was made to guarantee it is packed brimming with valuable information. Peruse, appreciate, take notes and then actualize — as that is the point at which the magic occurs.

CHAPTER ONE: WHAT IS THE CARNIVORE DIET?

The carnivore diet is presumably the most straightforward diet at any point conceived. The essential thought is to eat meat – and only beef for every meal. It is anything but a protein-based diet; it's a meat-based diet. That implies the dieter will need to eat bunches of greasy meats and maintain a strategic distance from plant-based proteins. Fat is the fundamental element for energy, while protein helps power the elements of the body while giving essential structure squares and crude material for slender muscle mass. All plant-based items like soy protein, pea protein, beans, and nuts are to stay away from. No fruits and vegetables are expended on this diet by any stretch of the imagination. There are a few many varieties in the carnivore diet – for instance, a few people expend a predetermined number of dairy items and allow for little quantities of carbs – while others are very severe and go zero-carb. In either case, your drink choices will likewise be carefully restricted – the vast majority will drink just water and, perhaps, bone stock.

Why choose the carnivore diet?

The thought behind the carnivore diet is basic – eat only meat. We'll investigate this in more detail later, including investigating side issues like whether you can eat dairy. Still, the general thought of the carnivore or zero-carb diet all things considered known is to dispense with carbs.

History of the carnivore diet

To start our plunge into the carnivore diet, how about we take a gander at what the expression "carnivore" indeed implies, as that can give you an away from what the diet itself will involve. "Carnivore" is a Latin-based word that generally means "meat-eater", which is the reason we use it today as a name for creatures that can just endure off protein, for example, huge felines or fowls of prey. While advocates for plant-based diets will push their perspectives dependent on natural conditions, sympathy for fellow animals, or some other cultural issue, the one certainty they frequently disregard is that meat has been urgent to humanity's endurance and development. A straightforward gander at the historical backdrop of our species is proof of this reality.

For centuries our diet didn't change a lot. At once, most social orders had diets that comprised as a rule of meat and little else. During those occasions, diseases that are very normal today didn't exist. Diabetes, coronary illness, malignant growth and a whole host of immune system diseases that are spinning out of control in our cutting-edge society were not in proof.

As archaeologists and anthropologists paw through hundreds of years of the chronicled information, it isn't likely that they have gone over a 3,000,000-year-old cookbook. However, by analyzing the remaining parts and artefacts of our inaccessible precursors, alongside the actualizes and tools they utilized, we know that the essential piece of their diet comprised of meat.

Now, you may be asking why you should mind what was eaten 3,000,000 years back or even 500 years prior so far as that is concerned. It is significant because we essentially have a similar DNA and body piece as our predecessors. If their bodies were more acclimated with meat than plants, it is verifiable that we, despite everything, have similar systems grinding away in us today. History discloses to us that meat was the fuel that allowed the human race to endure, but to develop in stature and advance in brainpower.

The meat was basic for our precursors diet because it was a significant way to get enough calories into every meal. They didn't have a customary three-meals-a-day plan and had no clue when or where their next meal was coming from. Meat gave them a calorie-thick food source that gave the store of energy they should have been sufficient for the following chase.

It was not until we have shown up in the horticultural time that our diet started to shift to incorporate more plant-based issue. Horticulture made it conceivable to have a steadier and progressively solid wellspring of food, and it was distinctly now that eating customary meals turned into the standard. Because of the primary agrarian unrest roughly ten thousand quite a while back, human diets started to incorporate increasingly more plant-based foods. To start with, the number of grains we ate were negligible. This was expected to the truth that innovation had not yet been imagined that would allow these plant-based foods to be moved to our tables with any normality. However, since the 1700s, there has been a continuous but consistent increment in plant-based foods highlighting in our diets. A decent piece of this new utilization is as carbohydrates and sugars.

During the 1700s, the normal individual expended around 4 pounds of sugar a year. During the 1800s, this number had expanded to around 22 pounds for every individual. Today, our utilization of sugar has expanded to someplace in the locale of 180 pounds of sugar for every individual consistently. That is essentially faltering.

This doesn't imply that we are for the most part eating sacks of Snickers bars or then again crusty fruit-filled treats. While those foods are intensely loaded down with sugar, most of the sugars we expend today are in structures that we are not in any case mindful of. According to the American Heart Association, the normal American expends around 22 teaspoons of sugar each day.

A great deal of these sugars are covered up in the foods we have been told are acceptable for our health. As you read marks that make statements like "entire grains", "heart-healthy" and "no additional sugar", you can be excused for trusting you are taking care of yourself and your family nutritious passage. But makers have figured out how to mask the fixings utilizing names you may not be acquainted with. There are at any rate 60 names for sugar that are allowed to be used on foods names.

You may handily perceive terms, for example, glucose or fructose and know what they are. Still, you may not be comfortable with sugars with names like Florida gems, Muscovado, Panela, Sorghum, Turbinado, Barley Malt, Dextrin, Dextrose, Diastatic Malt, Maltodextrin, Maltose, Galactose, etc.

At the point when you read food names, you will, in general, observe the large print at the front touting the assumed health benefits, while your eyes just miss words like these in small letters at the back. The final product? You end up devouring unmistakably more sugar than you at any point expected to or were even mindful of.

This sugar in our diets is notwithstanding the foods that as of now contain a great arrangement of natural sugars, for example, organic products. Nor does it incorporate any foods that rapidly convert into sugar in your digestive system, for example, white rice and pasta. It is just about an assurance that any handled foods you eat will contain some type of included sugar. Sugar is by all accounts in nearly all that we eat. Regardless of whether we understand it or not, this sugar over-burden is one of the most fabulous guilty parties in keeping us fat, apathetic, slow and sick. Clinical science has indicated it is a significant contributor to the advancement of diabetes, malignant growth and even dementia.

However, removing sugar from our diets is more complicated than one might expect. It appears if we do that, there won't be entirely left on our plate – except meat, which takes us a round trip back to the first diet that our progenitors ate (and blossomed with). Presently we should get down to the meat (pardon the play on words) of why the carnivore diet is so gainful.

Health benefits you can expect

There are numerous reasons why humans naturally need to eat meat. Not exclusively is it delightful, but we get a feeling of fulfillment from meat that we don't get when we devour other food. The surface it offers can't be impersonated when we expend vegetables and fruits. While the two of them are chewable food, meat gives our jaws an exercise when we eat it. But there are many reasons why we would instinctually need to go after that last drumstick over the table.

Protein power

We regularly go after meat because of its incredible taste and capacity to fulfill our hunger, but we likewise go after it because we need it at a cellular level. Nutritionally, meat is very high in protein. It is frequently alluded to as a "complete" food source because inside it are for the most part the fundamental amino acids the body requirements for health. At the point when you expend a sufficient stock of creature proteins, you won't have to take any extra dietary supplements to get what you need. You can't state that of some other food gathering.

Our bodies are comprised of around 20 percent protein. Since the human body isn't equipped for putting away protein, our diets must be wealthy in it. We need to discover food sources that give enough protein to continue us consistently.

The human body needs around twenty different amino acids, which can be used to manufacture proteins. These are classified into either basic or non-fundamental amino acids. The body is equipped for delivering the unnecessary amino acids all alone, but those that are basic must be obtained through the foods you eat. What's more, they should be procured in the correct proportions so a lot of one or too little can check the impacts of the others.

Animal sources of protein like fish, eggs, poultry and meat are significantly more firmly lined up with the protein your body needs. They contain all the fundamental fixings in the correct proportions, so your body gets all that it needs to function properly.

Plant proteins, while plentiful, are not as powerful in giving the body legitimate sustenance. They, as a rule, will give some amino acids but are inadequate in others. So you might have the option to get a plentiful portion of protein from foods such as beans, lentils and nuts, but you will at present need to look for other plant sources to get the total supplement of proteins your body needs. That is the reason veggie lovers and vegetarians so regularly need to take supplements.

Animal proteins are once in a while found without anyone else. Meat, for the most part, accompanies a large group of different nutrients fundamental for human life. So, notwithstanding the basic amino acids, you will likewise locate the following:

- Vitamin B12: from fish, poultry, meat and dairy.
- Vitamin D: from eggs, dairy and sleek fish.
- DHA (Docosahexaenoic Acid): an omega-3 unsaturated fat found in fish.
- Heme-Iron: generally discovered in red meat. This type of iron is consumed by the body more effectively than the iron found in plant-based foods. It is very viable in forestalling paleness, which can debilitate the body.
- Zinc: from meat, pork and lamb.

The bottom line is that meat contains predominant types of protein and fundamental nutrients which the body needs to endure and flourish.

These nutrients additionally contribute significantly to more readily muscle quality and improve your capacity to keep up it as you age. A standard course of meat makes a difference to forestall muscle misfortune as you get more established with the goal that you can keep up your level of perseverance and activity for far longer than you could something else. It additionally contributes to more readily bone quality.

Diets that contain an enormous extent of meat have sufficient measures of calcium, nutrient D, nutrient B-12 and omega-3 unsaturated fats, all of which contribute significantly to by and large bone health. Also, B12 advances better brain improvement in kids and oils the wheels of the neural system so that the brain capacities better.

Some may contend that you can get similar nutrients from plants, but there is a significant difference. At the point when you devour a plant-based diet, in request to get a satisfactory inventory of every one of these nutrients, you should take vita- supplements, which are synthetically made. These synthetic vitamins do not liken to the nature of natural nutrients you get from eating meat, nor does the body retain them as totally as natural food.

Better weight management

One of the most widely recognized reasons why people pick the carnivore diet has to do with dealing with their weight. If you go on the web and quest for "diets also, weight misfortune" you will locate a constant stream of opposing suppositions on the ideal approach to do it. One diet that is increasing a great deal of traction right now the ketogenic diet. Fundamentally the same as the carnivore diet, it works for weight misfortune by confining the measure of carbohydrates an individual expends, constraining the body into a condition of "ketosis". In ketosis, the body is creating "ketones", which constrain it to consume fat instead of glucose for its energy, in this manner the weight misfortune. The carnivore diet works on that equivalent reason just it is stricter regarding which foods are allowed. The ketogenic diet allows for certain carbohydrates on the menu, but the carnivore diet demands zero carbs.

A few investigations have been directed that taken a gander at how the low-fat confined calorie diet, the Mediterranean limited calorie diet, and the low- carb non-confined calorie diet performed. The outcomes were astonishing. In 95.4% of the members in these examinations, following two years, it was the low-carb non-limited calorie diet that yielded the best outcomes.

There is a lot of hypothesis concerning why this works. One hypothesis is that while you can eat more calories (non-prohibitive), the meat will, in general, be additionally satisfying what's more, accordingly, you naturally eat less. Essentially, you feel full speedier, so you devour fewer calories, which will contribute to all the more likely weight the executives. In expansion, you have all the more perfect energy so you will consume more calories also.

There is no doubt from a scientific perspective that there are numerous advantages to dispensing with carbohydrates and sugars from our diets. Indeed, even the natural ones. The health benefits are many. In addition to the fact that you get the basic proteins required for your body to work appropriately, but you likewise wipe out presentation to many hazard factors that are inborn in the substantial utilization of grains furthermore, sugar. Without the additional sugars, your blood glucose levels will be increasingly steady, you lower your odds of creating numerous autoimmune disorders that can cause agonizing aggravation all through the body, and you give your body a colossal increase in energy simultaneously. Any diet that is 100 percent animal-based is naturally going to give you increasingly fat, which will be substantially more fulfilling and satisfying than a plant-based menu. This improves hunger control.

Nobody truly appreciates starting to eat less. It just is by all accounts to what feels natural. For centuries, humans never needed to stop and consider their nutritional needs: they never needed to tally calories, and measure food divides. How they ate was natural and instinctual.

It tends to be debilitating and disheartening to consider all the little subtleties when following a specific diet system. That is the main reason some numbers of people are searching for an approach that is straightforward and simple to follow. At the point when you are on the carnivore diet, you don't have a bunch of factors to stress over, and you can still give your body all that it needs in practically every chomp. It is the sort of diet that, with a little control, can undoubtedly turn into a lifestyle because it is so naturally on top of what our bodies need and need. This makes adherence a lot simpler – and the diet you can adhere to is the diet that works!

Much more health benefits!

Eating meat is undeniably more fulfilling than you may envision. Because of its high-fat substance and thickness, your body will take more time to digest it than some other food gathering. At the point when you eat carbohydrates, your body rapidly utilizes them up, leaving you vacant and hungry and needing another thing to eat soon after that. The proteins found in meat need to experience various obstacles in your digestive system before they can be useful to you. This implies they take more time to separate, broadening when you become hungry once more.

Why most diets don't work

Since the time food turned out to be generally plentiful in human social orders, dieting has become an issue. Plentiful food has implied weight gain for an ever-increasing number of people, and this has been the situation particularly since the finish of the Second World War when handled carbohydrates started topping off-market racks. The clinical foundation aggravated things in any event when it got conned into accepting that animal fats were the issue, prompting weight addition and cardiovascular failures.

Numerous in the clinical foundation—doctors and nutritionists the same—despite everything purchase into this folklore.

Thus, the essential dieting plan set forward was to confine fat admission and tally calories. As such, the basic dieting plan was to starve yourself to death until you reached your objective weight.

This kind of dieting leaves people feeling bad-tempered and unsatisfied. Eating little segments of lean meat, heaps of void vegetables and sugar-spiking carbohydrates leaves you unsatisfied. More regrettable, such diets are challenging to follow. Dieters are encouraged to tally calories, which implies you must have access to a huge database of what number of calories are in what food and you need to monitor the amount of each food is devoured.

Some people become completely hypochondriac about it, heading off to the difficulty of overloading their food to the last gram. Profiting by this approach, different showcasing plans were built up that endeavored to simplify the process by allocating "focuses" dieters could checkup, so they realized they were Following the standards required to shed pounds. On these sorts of diets, people attempt to top themselves off by "brushing" on celery, Brussels sprouts or carrots as though they were a bunny. They expend repulsively tasting low-fat sweets attempting to persuade themselves that they can eat low calorie and low fat and still "have everything." The final product of these approaches for most by far of people is a disappointment.

Some may have the option to stay with it in the long haul and get more fit, but most people will wind up feeling starved, tired, and low on energy. Along these lines, what do they do? They go off the diet and wind up putting on much more weight than what they began with. Others find that their body goes into "starvation mode" also, slows its metabolism because of low-calorie admission, and weight misfortune remains subtle. The bottom line is that these kinds of approaches are excessively drunk. Who needs to invest their energy turning into a food master, knowing what number of calories are in each gram of celery or tallying up subjective point plans.

As of late, researchers have found that fat isn't the adversary of health as it was once thought to be. Specifically, immersed fat, a sort of fat found in animal items, used to be viewed as a significant hazard for coronary illness. However, over the previous decade, enormous examinations have exhibited that there is no connection between soaked fat and coronary illness. Rather, the clinical and nutrition networks are going to the slow acknowledgment that it's the sugar that is at the underlying driver of ceaseless western diseases. That incorporates coronary illness, stroke, metabolic syndrome, cancer, and conceivably Alzheimer's and other dementia-related diseases.

The carnivore diet is the solution

We should recap:

- Sugar/carbs cause weight addition and lead to diseases and health issues like respiratory failures and even cancer.
- Standard dieting including calorie limitation and low-fat leaves dieters feeling unsatisfied, prone to cheat or gorge, and feeling tired and healthy.
- Standard dieting includes confused plans like correctly checking calories or attempting to follow crazy point systems.

Likewise, already, people had a simple idea about food. The old thought is "it's the calories moronic." Nutritionists have since quite a while ago idea that calories consumed – calories eaten = weight misfortune. However, how the body works make it clear this oversimplified see isn't right.

You don't have to know the subtleties, but the basic explanation is eating sugar causes the arrival of insulin into your bloodstream, which drives abundance calories into your body fat. Eat excessively sugar, and you'll get fat. It's that straightforward. It's additionally imperative to understand that, in a general sense, all carbohydrates are sugar.

Some are orchestrated in complex manners – they are sugars fortified together to shape "complex carbohydrates." Those take more time to digest because the body needs to break them separated – to get at the individual sugar particles. But, at last, it's all sugar.

Why carnivore is better than other diets

The carnivore diet understands these issues because it takes out calorie tallying, is anything but difficult to follow, and lets you "diet" while getting sufficient measures of energy.

The carnivore diet tends to the entirety of the issues and inadequacies that a for every- child faces with different diets. For instance:

- Eating greasy meat is satisfying.
- You naturally eat what you need – since it's satisfying.
- Since you're fulfilled, the need and want to eat and cheat is dispensed with.
- Fatty meats give all the energy your body needs. You won't feel worn out, touchy, and low on energy. The bottom line is that you're not attempting to starve yourself to get in shape.
- Expending a diet with sufficient measures of fat drives the body into a fat-consuming state – so you'll consume body fat as opposed to add to it.
- The carnivore diet is very basic. Simply eat whatever meat you need. No convoluted plans are expecting you to tally calories; on the other hand, include focuses.

- Since the diet is basic, it's anything but difficult to adhere to. You'll consider eating a part short of what you would following a standard carb-stacked low-calorie diet.

Is the carnivore diet right for you?

The carnivore diet isn't really for everybody. A few people will essentially be reluctant to surrender carbs. But is the diet directly for you? Peruse on and choose for yourself.

Do you have a metabolic disorder?

Numerous people in present-day America experience the ill effects of a metabolic disorder. Essentially, this implies your body can't generally process carbohydrates the correct way. The foundation has named this as a disorder because they are still gotten up in the legend that eating a diet with enormous day by day servings of carbohydrates is ordinary. It isn't, but a few people have had the option to adjust to it. Huge numbers of us have not. All in all, how would you know if you have a metabolic disorder?

The primary piece of information is you've been slowly putting on weight as the years pass by. Regardless of whether you don't eat that much, getting your alleged "extents" right, you still wind up putting on weight. If you're approaching middle age, you'll progressively discover your paunch developing in size. People with the metabolic disorder are regularly pre-diabetic. This implies they'll have high fasting blood sugars, just not sufficiently high for an actual diabetes analysis. Your PCP may encourage you to "eat right" and get "some activity." You attempt this yet keep putting on weight.

An individual with the metabolic disorder, if they trouble to check, will find that they have blood sugar spikes after a run of the mill meal. While it's typical for blood sugar to go up an hour in the wake of eating a plate of spaghetti, somebody with the metabolic disorder will see theirs go up 20,

40, or more focuses when contrasted with a "typical" individual. This may be you if your blood sugar goes up more than 140 mmol/l an hour or two after a meal.

Another characteristic of metabolic disorder is high triglycerides. We'll talk progressively about triglycerides later, but if your fasting triglycerides are more than 100 mg/dl, at that point, you may have metabolic syndrome or be on the way to creating it. At last, hypertension is viewed as a part of metabolic syndrome. The bottom line is somebody with metabolic syndrome isn't too acceptable at digesting carbohydrates. If that portrays you, at that point, you may be somebody well fit a carnivore diet.

Would you like to improve body composition?

The fundamental impact of the carnivore diet on the vast majority is quick weight misfortune.

Besides, they are going to consume fat – and consume off their body fat. Thus, anybody hoping to pick up muscle and lower their level of body fat ought to consider a carnivore diet.

Are you serious about change?

While a carnivore diet sounds straightforward, and from multiple points of view, it will be, it additionally takes discipline. At the point when you choose to eat carnivore, enticements will be all around you. Perhaps your family concludes they would prefer not to follow your way and they're okay eating pizza, chips, and frozen yogurt. You will go to standard ties or host gatherings at the workplace brimming with cake and other sweet enticements. Cafés serving French fries and another carb treat consistently call.

You'll likewise need to fight the fact that your loved ones will presumably keep eating carbs and believe you're somewhat unusual for following this diet. Contingent upon whom you spend time with, the weight will be extraordinary. It might waver between people believing you're insane to straightforward joke for your dietary decisions. To face the hardship, you will be 100% genuine and focused on rolling out the improvements you have to make to lose weight and bring your body into a condition of genuine health and concordance.

It's one comment you're going to make a straightforward but extraordinary change and very another to do it. Are you genuine about weight misfortune lastly getting it right? Are you genuine about your pledge to weight misfortune and better health? While the standards of the carnivore diet are basic, actually following them throughout every day will be difficult from the start. If you're the sort of per- child who isn't not kidding about following through with large changes to improve your life, at that point possibly carnivore isn't for you. But if you've resolved to lose weight and get healthy for genuine this time, at that point, you ought to consider embracing the carnivore diet.

Can we say you are willing to put in the work?

The truth of the universe is there is no "free lunch." Getting brings about any undertaking takes difficult work. A great many people aren't ready to deal with it, and that is the reason a great many people get average or even terrible outcomes. To get results with the carnivore diet, you must be eager to place in the work.

The first few days will be a battle, but over the long haul and you break your sugar habit and indeed, we have gotten dependent on sugar simply like it's heroin or some other dangerous substance – you'll start to find that the work becomes natural and simpler to apply.

Meanwhile, contingent upon how dependent your body is to carbs, your experience may be pure hopelessness. You can get past it by keeping your ultimate objective as a primary concern and understanding that the despair is brief. For certain people, it very well may be especially extreme, while others adjust rapidly. If you're as of now doing low- carb, paleo, or even better keto, you'll most likely adjust quicker than somebody transitioning straightforwardly from the standard American diet weighed down with carbs. If the last-mentioned depicts your circumstance, you should go through about fourteen days to a month on a keto diet to slip into carnivore all the more no problem at all.

If you're willing to place the work in and carefully follow a carnivore diet for at any rate a month, at that point it's a diet that may work very well for you.

Possibly the carnivore diet isn't for you

There are a few people this simply won't work for. The most self-evident are veggie lovers and vegans. Indeed, we might be expressing the conspicuous since it's called the carnivore diet, but we have to get this off the beaten path. There is no form of this diet that works for veggie lovers. If you're veggie lover or vegan but are searching for a low-carb, moderate-protein, high-fat diet, you should investigate a veggie-lover adaptation of the keto diet – and they are out there. The carnivore diet depends on the rule that eating meat is fundamental to health. There essentially isn't a route around this.

While the carnivore diet is as close as you can get, particularly if you're pre-diabetic or experiencing metabolic syndrome, it is anything but a handy solution. If you're searching for a mysterious pill to soften the pounds away, this isn't your answer. We are a pill-fixated society and believe that we can continue doing the awful things we're doing while at the same time having a pill fix the unavoidable ramifications for us. It's most certainly not like that with the carnivore diet. It's a lifestyle change, not only a diet, and it requires duty. That doesn't mean you can't see once in a while cheat (more on that later), but for by far most of your everyday life, you will be concentrated on eating meat, and that's it. An enchantment pill lets you get the advantages without the work. That isn't the situation with this diet.

At long last, shut disapproved of people aren't welcome. Actually, if you raise the carnivore diet to a room loaded with people, the greater part of them are going to shake their heads and state, "that is insane!" Claims of sick health and passing will follow.

If you do a speedy Google search, you'll discover that a large number of people are most certainly not just getting by on a carnivore diet, they're blossoming with it. You can be shut disapproved and not have any desire to attempt a diet the foundation accepts is "radical" and indeed "perilous" – or you can try it.

In fact, at this moment, I am going to present a 30-day challenge. Simply attempt it – submit right presently to eat the carnivore route for a month. Focus on traversing the early good and bad times and then following a month, assess whether it's the privilege diet for you. If you accomplish the challenging work and stick to it for a strong month, you'll know if the diet is the correct one for you.

A few people may need to alter by doing keto or receiving a paleo-style diet – but you won't know until you attempt. And regardless of whether you do wind up embracing a more adaptable diet, you'll, at any rate, get the gigantic advantages that 30 days of carnivore eating will produce for your body, such as relieving your metabolic issues.

Activity: Go to a store and purchase a thick note pad, and begin keeping a food diary. On the principal page, note the following:

- Your present weight.
- Most recent fasting blood sugar, triglycerides, and HDL cholesterol.
- A sensible weight loss objective.
- List five reasons you should attempt the carnivore diet.

- List five issues with the carnivore diet – and then record why they don't concern you.

CHAPTER TWO: MYTHS ABOUT THE CARNIVORE DIET

Since the carnivore diet is seen as "radical" and "risky" by the foundation, there are a few legends that whirl around it. How about we experience these and see what's truly valid and what's not.

Eating only meat is bad for you

For a long while, the standard way of thinking has been that eating meat is awful for you – particularly red meat. And it's surprisingly more terrible if the meat is greasy. Doctors have since quite a while ago accepted that eating a great deal of meat causes heart attacks, stroke, weight increase, and cancer. It's even been proposed as a reason for appendicitis and gallbladder disease.

The individuals who consider what they're perusing may ask themselves a question – how is it that an animal type that developed on eating meat presently discovers meat to be a significant reason for disease? Does that indeed bode well? There isn't a single anthropologist who questions that our far-off precursors flourished with a diet that is wealthy in meat and fat and that this prompted bigger brain size. We likewise have rapacious teeth, and yet, many circumvent disclosing to us we ought to become vegetarians.

Most investigations that show eating meat is an issue are epidemiological contemplates. In a nutshell, this implies they overview a huge gathering of people and inquire them what they ate in the course of the last 3 or 5 years. While they might be fascinating at times, this kind of study has significant imperfections. Most importantly, an investigation that relies upon review like that can't be accurate. Do you truly review how frequently you've been eating steak in recent years?

Or then again, what number of servings of natural product you had each day? Likely not.

Epidemiological examinations are famously problematic and expect people to round out long structures that take after the sort of standardized test you get in secondary school or to enter school asking you things like how frequently you expended a ½ cup of ice cream in recent years. An epidemiological investigation is different from a clinical report. In a clinical report, you would actually put one gathering on a specific diet and have a "control gathering" that follows a different kind of diet or eats "whatever." Even in a clinical report, there are issues because you can't ensure people are truly following the diet they should. In any case, it's an improvement. None have discovered any proof that meat is hurtful.

The primary issue with dietary examinations is that there is an unending rundown of some factors, and it's difficult if not difficult to weed every one of them out and figure out what truly contributes to the results you're examining. This has been especially tricky when taking a gander at meat utilization. To put it, plainly examines that have taken a gander at people's meat utilization propensities included huge gatherings of people who had different tendencies too – like smoking cigarettes. Many were additionally habitually lazy people and drank liquor. Perceive how the issues include? It's tough to decide whether a steak eater who is smoking kicked the bucket from the steak or the stogie.

Besides, ketogenic and low-carb diets have just gotten on as of late. Most contemplate that have taken a gander at health results including meat utilization – no make that all investigations – were taking a gander at people who pretty much followed regular diets. In this way, people eating red meat were eating a cheeseburger and fries or on the other hand, a steak and heated potato. Along these lines, presently, we see when somebody in the investigation created diabetes and had a heart attack – the undeniable inquiry is was that the meat or the potato?

The standard way of thinking has been it was the meat, and doctors have been stupidly promising people to eat an ever-increasing number of carbohydrates! We see the results – significantly increasingly hefty people strolling around. The customary way of thinking is wrong.

With regards to tending to the perils of meat, two things continually come up – soaked fat and cholesterol. The issue here? That counsel is dead off-base. Devouring cholesterol in food has no impact at all on the cholesterol level in your blood. Think about what – the body needs cholesterol to work. And when you get some in your diet, your liver makes less of it.

Besides, while "the specialists" have been going around encouraging us to eat "healthy, lean cuts of meat," they neglected to take note of that the cholesterol substance of a wide range of meat is about the equivalent.

The second thing that routinely comes up with regards to meat utilization is the feared immersed fat. The equivalent Keyes study produced the thought that saturated fat is risky because your body essentially makes cholesterol out of it. People who are generally healthy can lower their cholesterol by inherently limiting soaked fat admission to under 20 grams every day. But the kicker is there is no rhyme or reason for you to do that.

Rather than asking whether immersed fat raises cholesterol levels, a few specialists with increasing presence of mind posed a different inquiry – does soaked fat utilization associate with an expanded danger of death and, specifically, with heart attacks and strokes? The information is in – and we'll get straight to the point – the appropriate response is no.

Animal meat, regardless of whether it's a hamburger, fish, pork, or duck, has loads of immersed fat in it (on account of poultry, for the most part in the skin). Immersed fat doesn't build the danger of heart disease or cancer, and along these lines, that is another negative mark against the thought that eating meat, including greasy meat, is perilous.

The following inquiry on people's brains is this – does eating meat cause cancer?

Once more, the appropriate response is no. Any "proof" that it does has been attached to unstable epidemiological examinations. Any affiliation that has been found has been frail and is regularly repudiated by the outcomes originating from different investigations. This hasn't halted the clinical foundation; they love making proclamations about the risks of meat, and despite the lack of genuine proof, they persistently issue declarations about the dangers of cancer from visit meat utilization.

Chargrilled, smoked, and handled meats aren't hazardous either. Nitrates and nitrites, specifically, have become food evil presences. But did you realize that these synthetic concoctions are available in considerable sums in numerous vegetables? Truly, it's valid healthy "superfoods" like celery and spinach contain these intelligent synthetic concoctions. You may inquire as to why your primary care physician is instructing you to eat to such extent spinach as would be prudent while dodging bacon and franks when they contain the same synthetic concoctions. Restoring with celery salt delivers similar synthetic compounds, but food manufacturers can name those foods "uncured" because celery salt is "natural." Some cases that even your spit contains a portion of these synthetic compounds.

The fact is they are all near and eating some "prepared" meats (as long as they have not many or no carbs) won't hurt your health. Nor is burn flame broiling your meat any more than chargrilling vegetables would. Presently, we've built up that eating meat, all by itself, isn't risky. Shouldn't something be said about eating just meat? To respond to this inquiry, we by and by going to this present reality, where loads of inborn peoples have been doing exactly that for incalculable hundreds of years. And think about what, there isn't any proof that is subsisting on a meat-just diet does any damage at all.

We've just met the Inuit. For ages, these people living close to the Arctic Circle have blossomed with a diet that is either included meat and fish or very about so. Foods expended incorporate numerous flying creature species, caribou, moose, salmon, cold roast, whale meat, and seal meat. Remember that these foods contain a lot of fat.

Other inborn gatherings all through the world have likewise subsisted principally if not only on diets of meat or meat and dairy. These models incorporate the Shockingly, discovering heart attack casualties among these gatherings where traditional diets are followed is very difficult if not outlandish. Some have guaranteed that these people are hereditarily adjusted to these diets; however, examines have demonstrated that when these groups adjust western-style diets, their paces of disease and stoutness ascend to coordinate those of their western partners. The bottom line is that no genuine proof has been discovered that eating meat is terrible for you or that solitary eating meat is awful for you.

You'll suffer from vitamin shortage

Probably the greatest fantasy is that by eating just meat, you'll have vitamin deficiencies. The inverse is valid much of the time. For instance, think about that vegetarian plant-based diets neglect to furnish the body with vitamin D, vitamin B12, and vitamin K2 – every one of the three of which is just accessible from animal sources. Research is demonstrating that vitamin D is essential for resistant health and different functions in the body and that having deficiencies in vitamin D can prompt genuine health issues, including expanded paces of contaminations and even cancer. We all realize that vitamin B12 is fundamental, but shouldn't something be said about vitamin K2? It turns out that it assists clean with excursion your supply routes, forestalling calcification and later heart disease. It ought to be noticed that vitamin K2 can be gotten from plant sources but just when they've been matured.

A few vitamins, similar to vitamin E, are more earnestly to drop by from meat alone. However, there are numerous animal-based sources of vitamin E, including salmon, goose, trout, and other seafood like crayfish. A significant fact glossed over by food babysitters is that vitamins and minerals are progressively bioavailable from meat sources. In plain English, that implies that the body has a simpler time digesting and utilizing them. This is because plants would prefer not to be eaten. Along these lines, they've created guarded procedures to help diminish their hazard, but that makes it harder for us to digest them and get at the nutrients. Basic plant structure additionally makes it harder to digest them (cellulose).

Subsequently, while you can get vitamin A from a carrot, if you're eating animal-based foods high in vitamin A like chicken liver, the vitamin An in the liver is far increasingly accessible. In this way, you'll have the option to get a greater amount of it, and your body can use out of a little measure of food expended. A simple 3-ounce serving of liver gives 305% of your vitamin An and 265% of your B12 needs. The liver is likewise an astounding wellspring of vitamin C. Along these lines, while you may at first believe you're going to run into significant health issues by staying away from oranges and different fruits and vegetables and get scurvy, you can get a lot of vitamin C from animal sources.

Meat sources additionally contain fundamental minerals like potassium and magnesium. A quarter-pound of cheeseburger gives 245 mg of potassium and 4% of your prescribed every day admission of magnesium.

So, you can get all the vitamins and minerals you need from animal sources. It's ideal for incorporating some organ meat to guarantee you get all the vitamins you need but remember that the liver has a limited quantity of carbohydrates in it (as put away starch called glycogen, which all animals incorporating humans have in their bodies).

You have to eat fruits and vegetables

Noticing the above facts – that you can get all the nutrients your body needs from animal sources alone – is causing heart attacks to swell all through different foundation "bodies" like the American Heart and Cancer Association. Those equivalent people additionally affirm we have to eat a "rainbow of hues" from plant food, in any event, 3-5 times each day if not more. Do you think your predecessors living during the ice age had the option to eat fruits and vegetables speaking to each shade of the rainbow on a day by day or even yearly premise?

If they didn't do as such for as far back as 2,000,000 years, does it bode well that all of an abrupt currently you're going to drop dead if you don't do it? We've just indicated that you can get all the minerals and vitamins you need by eating entire animal sources, even vitamin C from chicken liver even though you partner it with citrus fruits like lemons and oranges. Things being what they are, what exactly would we say we are getting from fruits and vegetables?

The advantages are questionable. Indeed, you can get numerous fundamental vitamins and minerals from plant sources like spinach. However, the inquiry for those intrigued by the carnivore diet is, do you need to get them from plant sources? The appropriate response is obviously no. Plants have contrived a few resistances they use to attempt to impede predators from eating them. For instance, numerous plants contain synthetic compounds called phytates, that meddle with supplement retention. That is one explanation that numerous vitamins and minerals are increasingly bioavailable when expended from animal sources.

We're frequently informed that you ought to eat heaps of fruits and vegetables to forestall cancer. Consider the possibility that the inverse was valid. Research that was at first begun in the 1920s and 1930s but was covered for a considerable length of time indicated that sugar is the reason for cancer. This is known as the Warburg speculation. As of late, this examination has been restored and even the Nobel Prize-winning pioneer of DNA, James Watson, is getting tied up with it.

Here's an enjoyment fact
Got gas?
It's from the carbs you're eating.

Your body experiences difficulty digesting plant-based foods, and along these lines, you need gigantic provinces of bacteria to do it. And what do bacteria do while digesting the food they produce gas. And it must turn out one end or the other.

Interestingly, our body is significantly readier to digest proteins and fats without much help. Along these lines, you'll produce considerably less gas than you will be when eating a standard American diet stacked up on wheat and sugar. You can even attempt this with your canine – feed your pooch a low-carb diet, and much of the time, it will fix gas issues. This carries us to fiber, which is non-digestible plant material that the scientific foundation accepts is indispensable to getting food through your body. If you're eating a diet with plant foods, there is some reality to that. But is it carefully fundamental? The appropriate response is no.

Recall every one of those meat-eating cultures we met before? How much fiber do you think the Inuit were getting from their traditional diet? The appropriate response is none at all or if nothing else none for around nine months out of the year.

You needn't bother with fiber to digest food. As we'll see later, you can remain "standard" by keeping up legitimate mineral adjusts in the body.

Some will find that when beginning on zero-carb, they have a ton of diarrhea. We'll speak progressively about this in a later section, but this outcome from a lack of fiber; fiber assists with retaining water in the colon. Transitioning to carnivore your colon needs to figure out how to assimilate more water than it's utilized to. This requires some investment, but we'll give a few hints that will assist things with improving later.

Your brain runs on sugar

The facts confirm that a lot of your day by day glucose admission goes toward "energizing" your brain. However, your brain can likewise work on "ketones," which are fat molecules that give energy when you're on a low-carb diet. Additionally, your body can make glucose with the goal that your brain gets all the fuel it needs.

WHAT? Indeed, you heard that right – in a procedure called gluconeogenesis, the liver will utilize protein to make the glucose your body needs to keep the blood glucose level at the least level it ought to be for endurance. That is a radical idea.

Consider it for a moment – you don't have to eat any carbohydrates. If your body needs them, it can make them out of protein that you eat. And as we'll see later, devouring overabundance carbs doesn't do anything except lead to fat on the body.

Energy levels will plummet

Some people accept that eating a meat-just diet will obliterate your energy levels. There is a trace of legitimacy to this case, and that reality makes it sound tenable. What is that trace of legitimacy? In the absolute starting point of a carnivore or low-carb diet, people have low energy levels as their bodies conform to burning fat instead of carbohydrates for energy. There are additionally different issues that emerge in the starting phases of the diet, including mineral deficiencies. But, on the whole case, the lack of energy people see is brief. When the body has cleaned out its glycogen stores, and you're in ketosis (i.e., burning fat for energy), you will end up having higher energy levels.

People have more energy level issues on a high carbohydrate diet. The explanation this happens is because of insulin/blood sugar spikes, which likewise cause different hormones to be discharged that make people tired and fractious.

You won't be able to work out

This is truly identified with the energy issue. Your muscles need glycogen for work out – but we've seen that the body can make the glucose it needs out of protein. Thus, while individual eating meat just diet will have diminished levels of glycogen stores (in the liver), they'll be sufficiently provided in muscle tissue. Secondly, your body needn't bother with glucose for energy – you can burn fat in the type of ketones to get all the energy you need. Albeit new carnivore dieters will encounter weariness, this is brief and handily cured as a rule.

Activity: Right now, we will persuade ourselves that we can get all the minerals and vitamins we need from eating animal sources. Make a rundown of vitamins and minerals you're stressed over and then record a rundown of animal sources (researching on the web or your favored technique) and the vitamins and minerals they contain. Give extraordinary consideration to organ meats like heart and liver just as different kinds of poultry and fish. Along these lines, you'll have a list on hand that you can reference to ensure you're getting all the nutrients you think you'll require on the carnivore diet.

Advantages of the carnivore diet

So far, we've seen that the carnivore diet is anything but difficult to follow and doesn't cause hurt. Presently we should proceed onward to the advantages.

Fat loss

Fat loss is one of the essential advantages of going on the carnivore diet – but be- product the impact of the diet will rely upon where you're beginning from. Not every person is going to see the same outcomes. Who benefits the most? If you've been eating a diet with something like half of your calories coming from carbohydrates, you're going to locate that a carnivore approach to eating is going to have an emotional impact. Examples of overcoming adversity can be discovered everywhere throughout the web – may be the pounds soften away.

If you're overweight and even pre-diabetic, you're going to see emotional changes and quick. In the main week, you'll presumably lose a ton of water weight, as the body exhausts out stores of glycogen. Review that glycogen is a sort of starch that your body stores in muscle and the liver. A glycogen molecule is attached to four water molecules, and so when you pull out a glycogen molecule to burn, you are courageous to dispose of. The glycogen in your muscles is utilized during exercise when you've removed carbs of your diet the glycogen in your liver is called upon as a crisis wellspring of glucose. It doesn't keep going long as it just gives a few hundred calories, but people frequently end up setting off to the restroom a great deal when they are disposing of that overabundance water.

A subsequent symptom that happens when you remove your admission of glucose is that your insulin levels will decay. The drop-in insulin levels advise your kidneys to free the body of abundance sodium. And what do kidneys do? They make pee, so abundance sodium (well the body sees it that way) is completed – so you'll lose much more water weight.

Following a couple of days, your body will change to burning fat instead of sugar. Your liver will make ketones which will utilize fat to assume the job of providing energy that used to be provided by glucose. This is the place fat loss starts. As opposed to having insulin advise the body to store abundance calories as fat, the converse occurs, and the body starts utilizing its fat stores to give energy. When this occurs, people keep encountering emotional weight loss. It's not unprecedented to shed 20 pounds over a brief period or to shed 7-10 pounds for every month and a seemingly endless amount of time after month until your body finds a workable pace set point.

Many people who've been overweight for quite a long-time wind up weighing what they did in school. Few people may have less emotional outcomes. For instance, if you're as of now on a keto diet, while you may, in any case, observe further advantages, you may not lose gigantic measures of body fat by exchanging. The one special case is the point at which you're in a level, and keto doesn't make you get more fit any longer. Going carnivore can kick off your weight loss.

Improved body comp

Everybody needs more muscle mass and less body fat. We've quite recently depicted how the carnivore diet will assist you with liquefying the fat away. Eating a carnivore diet can deliver better body organization – that is increasingly slender muscle mass and less body fat – given that you get satisfactory protein admission, but don't overcompensate It. On a carnivore diet, you shouldn't waste time with estimating or tallying anything – just eat until you're full and fulfilled, but you'll need to choose greasy Slices of meat to guarantee your fat to protein proportions are in the correct zone. If you eat a lean slice of meat, you may wind up actually hitting a level or even putting on weight. This is because the liver can make sugar out of protein. You maintain a strategic distance from this issue by eating generally less protein and moderately increasingly fat. As a practical issue, go for pork midsection instead of a lean pork flank or snatch that rib eye or extra rib before eating a lean cut of sirloin.

But be sure you get satisfactory protein too. This should be possible effects on the carnivore diet by essentially eating enough of the correct sort of meats until you feel fulfilled. Afterwards, we'll talk about working out, but accepting that you're getting enough protein and fat in your diet, at that point weightlifting or body opposition activities will assist you with expanding your muscle mass.

Forestalls metabolic disorders

The center of metabolic disorder incorporates high insulin levels, insulin opposition, and high blood sugar levels. Subsidiary impacts incorporate high triglycerides, more body fat, and hypertension, all of which increment the danger of heart diseases and stroke.

By receiving a carnivore diet, you can leave metabolic disorder speechless. This will put you out and about not exclusively to a lot of weight loss but likewise to better health. The carnivore diet does this by removing the fuel of metabolic disorder – which is a similar fuel for weight gain, and that is sugar utilization.

Improve mental clarity

For a considerable length of time, doctors have utilized ketogenic diets to treat youngsters with epilepsy. This is a clue that ketosis – the way toward burning fat as opposed to sugar for energy – most likely has health impacts on the brain. Specialists have additionally found proof that a ketogenic diet may assist fight with offing Alzheimer's, improve symptoms in Parkinson's patients, and may settle dispositions and mitigate gloom.

There's no uncertainty that ketosis benefits the brain. Scientists have likewise found that a ketogenic diet additionally improves mental lucidity and core interest. Regardless you're discussing with regards to the brain and diet, ketogenesis shows up to act on the brain in two different ways. The main way is immediate. Burning fat for energy is, by all accounts better for the brain. A few specialists guarantee that burning ketones is more energy proficient for the brain. For a given measure of fuel, you get a higher level of usable energy out of ketones instead of glucose. Ketones may likewise assist battle with liberating radicals in the brain and may even assist the ward with offing brain cancer.

However, essentially getting off carbs helps without anyone else. And it's anything but difficult to discern any reason why. When you eat a diet substantial in carbohydrates, your body is continually going through enormous high points and low points. In an hour or two in the wake of eating your blood pressure consistently increments. For certain people, it spikes to a truly elevated worth, making the hormones in your body vary with it to attempt to manage the circumstance. Your body discharges a lot of stress hormones putting you into a long run condition of irritation and "battle or flight" reaction.

While "battle or flight" may be useful on a mountain trail when you run into a cougar, it's bad for your everyday life.

The inescapable accident follows blood sugar spikes, and seething appetite later on a couple of hours after eating. It's anything but difficult to see how a diet wealthy in carbohydrates expects you to eat just to remain scarcely practical continually. There's no way crude people, who had sporadic access to food, could have worked along these lines.

At the point when you're continually stressed, and your blood sugar is going all over, it's difficult to remain mentally sharp. Center and focus become outlandish, and your critical thinking capacity disseminates. So even without the advantages that ketones themselves give as fuel, basically killing the good and bad times that accompany a diet loaded down with sugar is enough to improve your mental clearness. Albeit so far the proof originates from a keto diet, a carnivore diet can be considerably progressively compelling since you're going zero-carb.

Easy and effective

Most diets are unpredictable, with extensive arrangements of rules to follow. You don't know very what to eat or not eat, and followers continually contend about it. This is valid indeed, even with close family members of the carnivore diet, for example, paleo. While keto is less difficult than paleo, you despite everything need to give a ton of energy and consideration, making sure that you're getting every one of your macros right and watching out for carbohydrates.

Carnivore disposes of every one of these issues in a single shot. It's a straightforward and powerful diet that is the most effortless by a long shot to follow. Truly, there are a few varieties, and we will talk about those, but generally speaking, the guidelines are straightforward – drink water and eat meat. And it's ensured to work for everybody. If you're overweight, you are ensured to get more fit and improve your body structure by following a carnivore diet.

Activity: Look at your circumstance as it exists before you've gone on a diet. Record your best three objectives toward the beginning of your diary. Are you essentially attempting to get in shape, improve mental clearness, or fix health issues like metabolic syndrome? By defining specific objectives, you'll guarantee that you're effective with the diet.

CHAPTER THREE: THE SCIENCE BEHIND THE CARNIVORE DIET

It's a most likely sound judgment that eating just meat will prompt weight loss – given that you've liberated yourself from the standard folklores the medical foundation attempts to brainwash us with. But there is a study that backs up the essential standards behind the carnivore diet. We should investigate how and why it works. We'll go over the science behind the carnivore diet in an easygoing way so you can be educated without your eyes staring off into the great unknown. In all honesty, the carnivore diet was first given an account of in the nineteenth century, and you can peruse it online here, where a researcher depicts attempting meat just diet on themselves.

Most scientific information on carnivore lifestyles is observational, assembled decades back when anthropologists and doctors examined clans like the Inuit, who had a traditional diet that was practically 100% animal-based. Recent studies are difficult to find because the carnivore diet is generally new in the open psyche and just started picking up prevalence in recent years. In this way, for actual science, we're compelled to depend on the comparative keto diet. However, the outcomes are likely fundamentally the same as.

What happens when you eat carbs?

Eating a meal with any significant measure of carbohydrates promptly sets your body without hesitation. You may consider it is setting off alerts, although the body is intended to get energy from sugar. At the point when you eat carbohydrates, your blood sugar begins rising. Something should be finished with such sugar, so the pancreas discharges an intense hormone called insulin. The subtleties of how these works aren't too significant for the vast majority to know, you simply need to know two fundamental facts about insulin:

- It attempts to get cells to take up the blood sugar so they can utilize it for energy.
- Insulin makes the overabundance be transformed into fat and put away – as body fat.

For certain people, this works flawlessly fine, at any rate for some time. The proof is evident that as people age, this system starts to get broken in an enormous bit of the populace. A few people may scarcely see while others create pre-diabetes and out and out sort two diabetes. But what is one thing that a great many people in middle age share for all intents and purpose? Weight increase (stunning news!). One issue is that, after some time, your body gets impervious with the impacts of insulin. The state of insulin opposition implies that it will take more insulin increasingly to get a similar measure of blood sugar taken up by the cells as the years pass by. This will display in a few different ways:

- You'll have more and greater spikes in your blood sugar level after a meal. Perhaps five years back, your blood sugar crested out at 140 two hours in the wake of eating pizza, but today it goes as far as possible up to 180.
- You'll feel yourself slamming in the wake of eating carbs. You'll lack energy, and a few people may even feel temperamental or exhausted and need to take naps.

Your fasting blood sugar will be higher over the long haul. A1C – a test that measures normal blood sugar in recent days – will increment. If you're visiting the specialist, they may turn out to be somewhat frightened by your fasting blood sugar and/or A1C test results. But most doctors do the stupidest activity – they'll encourage you to eat entire grains. That's right – more bread, pasta, and other "entire grains." But don't be tricked, it's everything sugar regardless of whether the body needs to work a little to break it separated. Consider that – your body builds up an issue using sugar – and the medical foundation educates you to eat more concerning it.

Blood sugar

The carnivore diet steps in as a conspicuous solution to this issue. If eating a plate of pasta causes every one of these issues, why not simply quit eating pasta? And if vegetables like sweet potatoes and even kale contain carbs, why not kill them? It's a solution so evident that it's a marvel why it took such a long time for us to return to a style of eating that our ice Age predecessors knew. If you're just eating meat and fat – you're never going to have this issue – as a rule. There is one important admonition. Your body can make glucose. And it does this when you're not eating carbs. This is finished by making glucose out of protein. If you're not cautious, you can gobble a lot of protein and wind up having high blood sugars. This was exhibited by a popular carnivore diet advocate named Sean Baker – who is an MD. Pastry specialist ate carnivore for a significant stretch of in any event a year but never had his blood lipids checked. When he at long last did, it was uncovered he had a high fasting blood sugar and a high A1C value. Dough puncher's fasting glucose was 126 mg/dL – a level thought about sufficiently high by numerous doctors for a finding of type 2 diabetes.

Additionally, his A1C was 6.3 – once more, sufficiently high that most doctors may start by recommending a medication like metformin to control his blood sugar. He likewise had a fasting insulin of 2.6 ml/L. Cook is an active competitor, and some have theorized that his significant level of physical activity may be producing his glucose numbers, but that explanation isn't persuading. More than likely, he isn't getting enough fat in his diet and is getting an excessive amount of protein. And a portion of that protein is being changed over into blood sugar. For the record, Baker additionally announced a fasting triglyceride level of 54, which is viewed as healthy. Thus, don't surrender. The bottom line is if you're sensibly cautious and eat enough fatty cuts of meat and not all that much protein, the carnivore diet will get your blood sugar leveled out. If you find that it's not doing as such, investigate what you're eating and increment the fat while lowering the protein a tad and see what the outcomes are.

Decreased insulin resistance (insulin sensitivity)

We recently observed that, as your body becomes acclimated to sugar after some time, it becomes inaccessible with the impacts of insulin. This is called insulin opposition or then again, insulin affectability. If you're pre-diabetic, at that point there is no doubt that you're experiencing this issue, but fortunately, it very well may be reversed by just changing what you put in your mouth. Once more, your outcomes here will rely upon ensuring you don't try too hard on the protein. Ensure you're getting your energy generally from fat. It's really simple to do this – reach for the rib eye rather than the sirloin.

Or on the other hand, if you're eating chicken, eat the leg quarters rather than lean bosom meat. Insulin obstruction is straightforwardly identified with blood sugar issues. After some time, your body will modify. If you stun it by totally removing carbohydrates, after some time, your body will essentially fix itself, and your insulin obstruction will diminish. As such, your pancreas will have the option to complete a similar activity discharging littler measures of insulin.

What is ketosis?

The idea of driving ketosis is basic. When you quit eating carbs, gave that your protein admission isn't excessively expensive, your body will begin using fat for energy. It does this by having your liver manufacture chemicals considered ketones that you can essentially consider as the fat's solution to sugar's glucose. There are three sorts of ketones. You don't have to exhaust yourself realizing what they are, but the body doesn't utilize one (acetone), and it will be killed in your pee. The other two, however, can be used successfully for energy in place of glucose. They additionally cross the blood-brain boundary and so can be used to fuel the brain. If you've heard that the brain must have glucose for energy, that is off-base. However, your blood sugar is continually going to be kept up inside a restricted range to guarantee some glucose is accessible. As we've noted on a keto or carnivore diet, this is finished by making glucose out of a portion of the protein you consume.

Things to think about ketosis

- When you cut out carbs, it takes a couple of days to switch to ketosis. The body will burn through a store of carbohydrates; it keeps in the liver called glycogen.
- Some people behave more active than others at entering ketosis.
- You can get all your energy needs fulfilled by fats while on ketosis.
- When you're getting energy from ketosis, the body naturally burns your body fat for energy, causing weight loss and improved body composition.

- Eating an excessive amount of protein can restrain ketosis.

Presently, people on the ketogenic diet can be neurotic about ketosis and even go around with minimal electronic meters constantly pricking their fingers to discover what their level of ketones is. It's not necessary to be that point by point on a carnivore diet. Simply follow these straightforward guidelines:

- Eat until you're fulfilled. If you have an inclination that you have to eat more, do it. Try not to continue eating if you feel satiated.
- Drink adequate amounts of water.
- If you locate that over a significant period, at any rate, a month, you're not shedding pounds, at that point eat somewhat less protein and slightly more fat.
- Select fatty cuts of meat.

Reduce triglycerides

If you search on the web, this effect is demonstrated again and again anecdotally. Carnivore dieters uniformly observe their triglyceride levels drop by enormous edges. Visit your companion Google and search for carnivore diet and triglyceride level to see people's outcomes. As a rule, a fasting triglyceride level below 100 is acceptable - the lower, the better. You'll see that long haul carnivore dieters will, in general, have triglyceride levels between 50-80. This effect has been demonstrated in a few distributed examinations which have looked at the health impacts of severely restricting carb consumption through the ketogenic diet. One such paper that was distributed in 2004 was entitled "Long haul effects of a ketogenic diet in obese patients." This investigation found that fasting triglyceride levels dropped a fantastic 60% among study participants. For what reason is this significant? Because high triglycerides are a significant marker for increased risk of heart disease. The proportion of your triglyceride to HDL level is considered by most cardiologists to be the most significant blood lipid marker in deciding the future risk of a heart attack. By and large, levels greater than 2 are at increased risk, and the higher the number, the higher your risk. Up to this point, it wasn't generally gotten why – but high blood triglycerides bring about thickly packed LDL or "terrible" cholesterol molecules. Being littler, they can stick in corridor dividers, prompting the arrangement of plaque and inevitable heart disease that could bring about a heart attack or stroke. High triglycerides can likewise cause different genuine health problems, such as increasing your risk of pancreatitis, a conceivably destructive inflammation of the pancreas the same as with heart disease, the higher your triglyceride level, the higher your risk.

Anyway, what causes high triglycerides? Most doctors who haven't stayed aware of re-searching that fat in the diet causes it. They are dead off-base, and this has been demonstrated in a few investigations. One research assembled a group of 16 people and had them increase their carb admission for a while. It was discovered that, before the finish of the investigation time frame, their triglycerides had significantly increased, and they had created different problems like "fatty liver," which can cause liver disappointment after some time. Alcohol can likewise cause high triglycerides, especially if you consume a huge sum over a brief period. That is the reason substantial consumers are at increased risk of pancreatitis.

The bottom line? Eating sugar/carbohydrates raises your triglyceride level. That develops your risk of heart disease and other health issues. A diet dependent on meat and fat will dramatically lower your triglyceride level, decreasing your risk of heart disease.

Improved cholesterol

The proportion of triglyceride/HDL cholesterol is the best marker for heart disease risk. The lower that number is, the better. You can lower it by lowering your triglycerides or by raising your

HDL. However, those numbers will in general move together. People with high triglycerides regularly have low HDL, which is a piece of "metabolic syndrome." Although formal investigations of the carnivore diet haven't been done, the examination we referenced before from Experimental Clinical Cardiology "Long haul effects of a ketogenic diet in obese patients" found that patients following a low-carb ketogenic diet raised their HDL cholesterol by a normal of about 22%. Direct outcomes from carnivore dieters so far are anecdotal. Still, a few people have announced HDL going up more than 100, which is an exceptionally high value and accepted to be incredibly protective. Assessing the anecdotal information, it creates the impression that all carnivore dieters will see significant reductions in triglycerides, but just some will see huge increases in HDL. A few people are simply genetically wired to have low HDL numbers if that is you don't stress over it if your triglycerides are below 100.

Why high total cholesterol isn't necessarily bad

For as long as 50 years, the public has been brainwashed to accept that high all out cholesterol is hazardous. The fact is it's not. There are a few reasons why this number without anyone else is insignificant:

- A sheltered cholesterol value is accepted to be below 200. However, half of the first heart attack victims have all-out cholesterol numbers below 200.
- HDL is a piece of your complete cholesterol number. If it's high, your complete cholesterol number might be high without truly meaning anything.
- Total cholesterol can't be seen in confinement. Your triglyceride number should be known.
- If you have a low triglyceride to HDL proportion (under 2, by and large), at that point, this indicates your LDL or "terrible" cholesterol isn't generally an issue.

- LDL is extremely just "terrible" cholesterol when you have a high particle number, and the particles are little and thick. That implies they can stick to blood vessel dividers, causing heart disease. If you have a low LDL number and the particle size is large (some state huge and cushioned) at that point, they won't stick to your blood vessel dividers and cause disease.
- Many blood lipid tests don't check for this, but you can surmise the LDL

Why no plants?

The principal thing to note about plants is they contain carbohydrates with the goal that's the first and most evident answer why you don't eat plants on a carnivore diet. But there are different motivations to maintain a strategic distance from plants. A second motivation to cut out plants is plant-based foods regularly cause sensitivities in people. You may not be completely conscious of it- possibly you have aching joints, acid reflux that never shows signs of improvement or post-nasal drip around evening time that you've never associated with your diet. While strictly you ought to eliminate all plants from your diet for a carnivore, for the individuals who can tolerate it they can incorporate a modest quantity of seasonings and even sauces or condiments as long as they are low-carb. A model could be mustard. The key here is to investigate and see what works for you. For two weeks of the diet cling to a rigorous everyday practice of zero-carb all meat, and at that point, if wanted, you can include modest quantities of seasonings or sauces. If you select to add vegetables back in, at that point, you'll be on a keto, not carnivore diet. The fact is plants would prefer not to be eaten. So they've built up a lot of strategies to protect themselves from being eaten by animals. Plants contain numerous chemicals that repress the retention of the nutrients they contain. Powerful husks and shells protect multiple seeds. One problem with plants is the protein they contain. This is especially valid for wheat. The proteins from grains are inflammatory. You increase the risk of a wide range of chronic diseases when you're in an inflammatory state. For certain people, it's very dramatic, and they create problems like an inflammatory inside disease. In others, it may be significantly increasingly unpretentious, but the harm is similarly genuine. Probably the most significant factor in the improvement of heart disease is inflammation, and it is estimated by markers like C-Reactive protein (next time you complete your blood work, make certain to request a CRP test-an outcome not exactly or equivalent to 1.0 is alluring). A high C-reactive protein value implies your body – and your blood vessels – are aggravated. So perhaps you can eat pizza and pasta and don't have attacks of diarrhea – but you're despite everything harming your body in a progressively unobtrusive and similarly if not increasingly hazardous style.

Autophagy

We'll discuss this more in the context of fasting but going into a zero carb diet and entering ketosis can trigger a process called autophagy. In a nutshell, it implies your body is eating itself, but don't be frightened. It doesn't eat the great parts; autophagy includes what you may describe as taking out the junk. Much the same as getting the refuse out of your home makes it progressively bearable; autophagy can improve your health.

Activity: Complete your blood lipids, and if conceivable, get the most comprehensive test accessible. If your insurance doesn't cover it but you have a free facility in your location like "Any Lab Test Now", and you can bear the cost of it, at that point get the most comprehensive lipid board accessible. In any event, discover the following:

- Total cholesterol
- HDL cholesterol
- Triglycerides
- Fasting blood sugar
- A1C value
- CRP or c-reactive protein.

Write down your values in your diary. At that point retest in the wake of being on carnivore for an all-encompassing timeframe (at any rate 60 days, 90 is better) and retest, and compare values to record progress.

Carnivore versus paleo and keto

There are some low-carb diets out there, from Atkins to South Beach to Paleo. Carnivore is characterized as zero-carb, but how is it extremely different from other well-known diets that restrict carbohydrates? How about we look at the two most well-known diets – paleo and keto.

How is carnivore different from paleo?

You may state the reason for the zero-carb or carnivore diet is that notwithstanding maintaining a strategic distance from the documented problems with high-carbohydrate diets we should attempt to eat a diet as comparable as conceivable to what our ancestors ate. This is likewise the premise of the mainstream paleo diet also. Disciples of the paleo diet accept that our tracker gatherer ancestors ate a diet consisting of meat, vegetables, natural product, fish, eggs, nuts and seeds, and healthy fats and oils. Since conditions that tracker gatherers lived in shifted generally, there is a single nobody diet that can be said to look like a diet consumed during the Paleolithic time (where the diet gets its name). Still, the diet leaves out processed foods including cultivated grains like wheat. So with this, it may be considered to be generally accurate.

On the paleo diet, there is a general rundown of foods that most practitioners hold fast to:

- Grains – no bread, pasta, etc.
- Legumes – no beans, lentils, peas.
- Processed foods – stay away from processed meats, packaged snacks.
- No vegetable oils, albeit olive oil is considered acceptable by most. Soybean oil, sunflower oil, corn oil, and canola oil are prohibited from a paleo diet.
- Sugar and soda pop.
- Fruit juice drinks.

- Margarine. Some likewise replace butter with "ghee" while others approve of the utilization of butter.
- Artificial trans fats.
- Most dairy products.

Some followers do allow the consumption of full-fat assortments of milk and cheese – but obviously, tracker gatherers didn't consume these things. Low-fat things are strictly precluded. We see from this rundown that the denied foods on paleo are additionally restricted on the carnivore diet. Therefore, switching back and forward between the diets may be a possibility for some to seek after, and we'll consider that in detail later, but the paleo diet allows the consumption of numerous carbohydrates that make it drastically different from the carnivore diet. It's additionally increasingly complicated, and although you could see eating out as conceivable on a paleo diet, even that is progressively complicated. It's truly simple to go to 99% of eateries and request just the meat, but with paleo, there is a wide range of qualifications that must be considered. Most paleo practitioners allow the consumption of high-carbohydrate things that would completely invalidate the point of a carnivore diet. Followers of paleo accept that use of fruits and root vegetables is acceptable, on the conviction that tracker gatherers in the Paleolithic period consumed these things. This is flawed of course – during the ice age fruits and berries, in any event, would be challenging to find a large portion of the year. Regardless, the following things are considered acceptable to eat day by day (although the amounts may be restricted) on paleo:

- Sweet potatoes
- Carrots
- Blueberries
- Strawberries
- Apples, bananas, and other sweet fruits like oranges (note however that some paleo followers keep away from since these are cultivated fruits from the advanced time)
- Yams and turnips

- Avocados
- Alcohol with some restraint
- Salt and pepper and spices are allowed.

Some may utilize simple condiments like rubs. As a rule, these things could be healthy. They indeed contain a lot of nutrients, but the nutrients – even vitamin C – can be gotten from animal sources where they are increasingly bioavailable (simpler to digest and assimilate). The bottom line with the foods on this rundown, however, is that they will raise your blood sugar by enormous amounts. Eating any of the foods on this rundown will completely invalidate the point of the carnivore diet. Paleo additionally allows the consumption of nuts and seeds, which isn't something you will eat on the carnivore diet. While generally nuts and seeds people eat today are cultivated assortments that were not around during Paleolithic occasions, it's presumably accurate that tracker gatherers ate nuts and seeds when they were accessible. And more often than not, they were likely not eating these things. With regards to meats, the paleo diet fits in very well with food things eaten on a carnivore diet. Paleo practitioners are enthusiastic about eating grass taken care of and unfenced assortments, as these most closely take after the free-roaming animals eaten by Paleolithic tracker and gatherers. While buffalo or wild ox would be ideal, grass-took care of and completed meat is perfectly acceptable. Lamb, pork, and exotic meats are additionally allowed on a paleo diet as are poultry of any sort and seafood. Exotic meats like elk are additionally allowed. Wild-caught fish is liked, and salmon is a major staple on most paleo diets. Paleo additionally allows the consumption of eggs. Many favour omega-3 containing eggs, but it's difficult to perceive how that is truly something that existed during Paleolithic occasions, but it's a healthy choice. On the carnivore diet, a few people do consume eggs, and since they are zero-carb, they're certainly allowed.

How is carnivore different from keto?

Presently, we should consider the keto diet, which over the recent years has vault-ed ahead to become one of the most mainstream diets around. The keto diet restricts numerous foods that paleo doesn't, and so is significantly closer in soul to the carnivore diet. The keto diet isn't generally founded on thoughts regarding what tracker gatherers ate; its establishment is just founded on restricting carbohydrates. A keto diet underlines getting a large portion of your calories from fats and restricting protein consumption. Still, on a carnivore diet, most advocates exhort eating both protein and fats generously. All things considered, if it's not too much trouble know that if you're eating a great deal of protein on a carnivore diet but not getting more fit, you may need to rebalance by eating progressively fat with your meals. While numerous practitioners of the carnivore diet underscore zero-carb consumption and stick to red meat for simplicity, if you see the diet as essentially being constrained to animal products, some carb-containing products may be possible on a carnivore. Models include full-fat milk and yogurt. Note that these kinds of foods are not reasonable on a keto diet. A keto diet is more restrictive than paleo, but it allows the consumption of the following foods that are not allowed on a carnivore diet:

- Low-carb fruits like avocados and olives.
- Any vegetable that develops over the ground; common instances of vegetables consumed on a keto diet include spinach, kale, broccoli, cauliflower, cabbage, asparagus, and celery.
- Alcoholic drinks are allowed if they are low-carb. Along these lines, for instance, wine or vodka and soft drink are allowed, lager isn't.
- Low-carb berries are allowed with some restraint such as blackberries or strawberries, although dieters who follow a stricter routine won't eat these.

- Nuts and seeds might be allowed in exceptionally little amounts.
- Sauces and condiments are allowed if they are without sugar or low-carb.
- Spices are allowed. A keto diet bans the following things (a considerable lot of which are allowed on paleo):
- Any grains. No bread, pasta, rice, quinoa.
- No legumes, so no peas, beans, or lentils.
- Soda and natural product drinks.
- Artificial sugars are kept away from or consumed in exceptionally restricted amounts.
- Apples, oranges, bananas and other sweet fruits are strictly restricted.
- Any vegetable that develops below ground isn't allowed. Not at all like paleo, the keto diet bans sweet potatoes, carrots, and turnips and of course, regular potatoes.
- High-carb and sweet alcoholic beverages are prohibited (brew, margaritas, white Russians)

- Milk, including full-fat milk, is prohibited because of lactose content.
- Sauces and condiments that contain sugar are not allowed.

A keto diet typically restricts carbohydrate consumption to 20-50 grams for every day. A few varieties of the keto diet are strict, sticking at 20 grams, while others allow more variety or time-constrained changes. A case of this is the Atkins diet which restricts every day carbohydrate consumption to 20 grams for each day but then allows higher consumption of carbohydrates from that point.

The keto diet places strict cutoff points on macros other than restricting carbohydrates. When following a keto diet, you should get in any event 70% of your calories from fats, and 80% is prompted. The main purpose of this restriction is that the liver can transform proteins into glucose utilizing gluconeogenesis. The fundamental thought of the keto diet is to be in a state of ketosis, where glucose isn't utilized by the body as fuel. With regards to meats and seafood, anything is allowed, including processed meats. While many exhort eating grass-took care of and unfenced assortments, this isn't generally part of the diet. Allowed foods include:

- Beef – fatty cuts are liked
- Chicken
- Turkey
- Duck and some other poultry
- Salmon
- Tuna
- All fish – trout, sardines
- Any seafood such as mussels, crab, lobster, shrimp
- Exotic meats like elk, venison, ostrich
- Dairy is allowed but restricted to extremely low or no-carb assortments.

Overwhelming cream is allowed, butter is allowed, and cheese is allowed, but any milk products or creamer are not allowed. Once more, the main restriction here is that fat ought to be the primary piece of the meal. Along these lines, on a keto diet, if you eat scallops or shrimp, you should most likely finish them off with an overwhelming cream sauce and loads of butter.

Advantages and disadvantages of carnivore over paleo and keto

The carnivore diet is far simpler to follow than paleo or keto. It's truly easy to say eat meat and nothing else as opposed to experiencing not insignificant arrangements of allowed and restricted food things. The keto diet likewise experiences the complexity of figuring your macro proportions at each meal and ensuring that the fat content is 70-80%. In all honesty, it's regularly difficult to concoct meals that meet such a specific restriction. In contrast, the carnivore diet doesn't specifically focus on that and suggests that you eat meat and eat what fulfills you. Just in uncommon cases is that going to cause problems with glucose, a great many people will increase all the advantages by wiping out carb-based foods from their diet. To outline, the professionals of the carnivore diet as compared to the paleo and keto diets are:

- Simplicity
- No compelling reason to calculate macros Only one precluded thing – plant foods.
- Avoid the drawbacks of eating plant foods that are still there when eating any sort of nut, natural product, or vegetable paying little mind to carb content.

Those who advance the paleo and keto diets would contend that vegetables (and fruits and berries, on account of paleo) are a fundamental piece of a healthy diet. The evidence on this is blended, and for a great many people, it will involve individual taste. Completely abandoning fruits and vegetables won't be for everybody and those people investigating a keto or paleo diet may be to their greatest advantage. However it should be said that so far, in any event, there is little evidence that is completely dispensing with fruits and vegetables has any health impact at all, and numerous people, especially those inclined to weight gain and blood sugar problems on a standard diet will profit the most following such an approach. Cons of choosing carnivore diet as compared to paleo and keto:

- You might be surrendering some nutritional advantages of fruits and vegetables, although, right now, there truly isn't evidence of that.
- Paleo and keto diets are all the more effectively versatile to social circumstances and eating out.
- Paleo and keto are all the more socially acceptable; eating carnivore may make them brand you as a radical.
- For certain people, digestive issues are all the more effortlessly managed on paleo and keto. On paleo, there are likely no digestive issues by any stretch of the imagination, and on keto, a lot of plant fiber is consumed. Hence, people acclimate to it more effectively than they will to going carnivore strictly.

After your goals are achieved, you can switch back and forth

How about we consider the principal low-carb diet that became famous, the Atkins diet. The Atkins diet is ketogenic; however, it's not as restrictive as the diets presently named as "keto." The main restriction on the Atkins diet is to restrict the number of carbs consumed every day, macro proportions, and demanding that fat be 70-80% of the diet is not so much considered on Atkins. Another aspect of the Atkins diet is that it proceeds in stages. In the induction stage, the Atkins dieter should go through around about fourteen days constraining day by day carb admission to 20 grams for every day. From that point onward, they can increase the measure of carbs consumed every day and can even reintroduce carb-based things to their diet, given that they don't cause recharged weight gain. The thought is to discover foods that you can eat in frequency and amount that work for you after you're reset your body and lost weight. You can likewise come back to the induction stage varying. A comparative approach can be utilized with the carnivore diet. Since there is no official diet dependent on this principle, you can attempt what works for you, but as a proposal, you can plan your own "induction stage" where you just eat meats for about fourteen days or a month. At that point, you can slowly progress to keto by introducing over the ground and low-carb vegetables or even change to paleo if that works for you. Between the choices of paleo and keto, keto is far simpler to progress with the carnivore diet. You can without much stress switch back and forward among carnivore and keto all the time. This is a strictly singular decision that each per-child should address for themselves.

Carnivore can assume a job inside the keto diet also. Numerous keto dieters start with incredible success, losing a ton of saying something the start. But, at that point, they hit an inescapable "slow down" where further weight loss becomes tricky. Right now, a 2-multi week carnivore stage can help kick off weight loss. The greatest issue with transitioning between keto/paleo and carnivore will be digestive problems. This will be, to a lesser degree, a factor with keto. Still, the elimination of the dietary fiber that you'll jump on a keto diet is as yet going to cause problems for certain people, which can include constipation or diarrhea.

Activity: If you are keen on utilizing the carnivore diet in conjunction with another diet approach like keto or paleo, plan your own stage-based diet utilizing the carnivore diet as your induction stage.

- Schedule a fourteen-day block (or as long as a month) where you just eat a carnivore diet.
- In the following two weeks, create a rundown of veggies, you will steadily add to your diet. Start with extremely low-carb assortments like asparagus.
- Track your weight like clockwork to guarantee to reintroduce food items isn't causing weight gain if you notice consistent weight increase throughout at any rate

seven days, at that point back of the most recently included food items.

- Your change can continue the extent that you like. For the individuals who favor the greater assortment of a paleo diet, you can continue step by step, including back food items, including higher-carb items like sweet potatoes and decide how they impact your weight.
- If you'd truly incline toward being on a keto or paleo diet over the long haul, build up a schedule that incorporates 2-week times of carnivore dieting to reset your system.

Incorporate flexibility with your routine

At the point when your diet consists of eating just meat, there is no uncertainty that at first, it can get exhausting quickly. It causes first and foremost to have one day in the week to go off and eat whatever you need. This will remove much of the stress from such a constrained diet, but won't do you any genuine harm. If you discover you miss the taste of your preferred veggies, choose to have them on a flex day. Or perhaps you just cannot avoid getting a slice of cheesecake when you are out with your companions. Spare that benefit for an occasional flex day to keep life somewhat more endurable at the start. Ensure that you schedule your flex day as opposed to moving it around randomly simply. For instance, if you have decided to have your flex day on a Saturday but when Saturday moves around you are not inclined to go off the diet, don't accept that now you can have it on Sunday or Tuesday. Rather, understand that if you don't go flex on Saturday, you should hold up until the following Saturday to enjoy. This will shield you from losing your cadence so you will stick to the program for more. Keep in mind, in the end, we need to eliminate flex days through, and through so you are 100 percent carnivore and receiving the full rewards of the diet. No doubt about it, going from a standard present-day diet to eating exclusively meat will speak to a challenge, but if you can execute these different strategies, you will find that creating the progress will be much simpler. The hardest piece of the carnivore diet is the beginning. So the greater the amount of these tips you actualize toward the start, the quicker you will change by your new nutrition plan. Once you are through the modification time frame, it ought to be much smoother going.

CHAPTER FOUR: BEGINNING ON THE CARNIVORE DIET

(The Basics) – In this chapter, we'll spread out the specifics of the carnivore diet. Compared to different diets, it's extremely basic, but we'll additionally address common problems that dieters will in the general encounter. Remember that the difficulties people encounter are transitory as your body acclimates to another method for eating. Before we proceed with our rundown of foods you can eat, it's imperative to take note of that numerous practitioners to follow the least complex program conceivable – they simply eat red meat, and that's it. Shawn Baker, who is one of the main advocates of a carnivore diet, just eats rib eye steaks. Dough puncher has stated that he does this for simplicity and to make it simple to follow, not for strictly nutritional reasons although rib-eye steaks do fulfill that. You can follow a program this way and jump to the following chapter. However, it is conceivable to have a shifted diet while as yet eating "carnivore," and along these lines, we give a nitty-gritty rundown of foods you can eat. The general thought is to eat animal-based foods. Many like to be strictly zero-carb, but that isn't necessary either (and remember that liver contains carbohydrates, as glycogen – but as an animal product packed with vitamins and minerals, it is a decent expansion to the diet). The assortment you include or don't include in your diet involves individual taste.

Foods you can eat

While the carnivore diet is regularly described as a meat-eating diet, it is increasingly accurate to state that the diet consists of eating animal-based products alone. Since no carbohydrates are consumed by any means (at any rate plant-put together carbohydrates – more concerning that in a moment), fattier cuts of meat are liked. Everybody realizes that rib-eye steak is increasingly "hearty" than a chicken bosom, so that is the basic guide that ought to be utilized in selecting your cuts of meat. While it is sheltered to state that any sort of meat is allowed, how about we get increasingly specific with the sorts of foods you can eat on a carnivore diet.

Meats

The essential meat source on a carnivore diet is red meat. For most, this implies hamburger, but you can likewise eat buffalo/wild ox and include some progressively exotic meats in your diet. The essential cuts of hamburger that are favored because of their higher fat content are rib eye, New York strip, and T-bone. Porterhouse steak and prime rib are likewise excellent choices. Different sorts of hamburger, including ribs, roast meat, and flank steak, are acceptable choices. Ground meat/burger is certainly allowed (without anyone else – no buns) but chooses higher-fat assortments (80/20 or 73%). Leaner cuts of meat like sirloin can likewise be consumed, but you would prefer not to eat a meal that is for the most part protein. Lamb is an extraordinary choice. If you eat a meal with a lean cut of meat at that point back it up with some fat – for instance, include some bacon. Simply eating a lean cut of meat won't be fulfilling for a great many people, and it won't assist you with keeping up a state of ketosis.

Poultry

Poultry is unquestionably allowed, including chicken, duck, turkey, geese, and wonderful. Fattier cuts are liked. In particular, chicken and turkey bosom are lean so add additional fat to your meal if that is what you're eating. The skin ought to be consumed to get the fat. Chicken thighs, legs, and wings are excellent choices. If you can discover it and manage the cost of it, duck bosom is probably the best choice for poultry since its moderately high fat and exceptionally fulfilling.

Processed Meats

Processed meats can be consumed on a carnivore diet. While to some degree, the premise of the carnivore diet is following a diet that our ancestors ate (in any event in certain circumstances), the genuine objective is to keep away from carbohydrates. In this way, processed meats can be a piece of your diet. However, it is important to be very careful in selecting your processed meats because numerous contain carbohydrates. If your objective is just to keep away from plant foods, this most likely won't be an issue because the level of carbohydrates is typically extremely little. But if you're doing zero-carb, at that point, you'll need to be amazingly careful in selecting any processed meats. Discovering high-fat assortments isn't an issue; frankfurter, sausages, salami, for instance, are for the most part high in fat. If you're on a careful spending plan, consider items like Vienna hotdogs – they have trace amounts of carbohydrates but have high fat and moderate protein content, so they are useful for ketosis, also exceptionally low-cost. Hotdog is an incredible food to include but consistently check carb content. A few manufacturers of frankfurter include more carbs than others.

Organ meats

Organ meats are extraordinary to include in your carnivore diet. Probably the greatest advantage of including organ meats is that they are loaded with vitamins and minerals your body needs, such as vitamin An and even vitamin C. The two top picks are liver and heart (chicken and hamburger are both acceptable sources). Chicken gizzards are likewise acceptable to eat. There aren't any cutoff points, so you can eat anything you can tolerate from the brain to the tongue (the tongue isn't an organ, but it's somewhat exotic for most Americans)

Exotic meats

Here, we include meats that aren't regularly a component of the standard American diet, although it is calling them "exotic" is most likely a stretch. You can eat gator, elk, kangaroo, hare, venison, and wild hog, for instance. However, note that huge numbers of these meats are incredibly lean. In this way, if you will have a meal where this is the fundamental serving, make certain to include some fat.

Eggs

Eggs can be securely consumed on a carnivore diet, and you don't need to restrict yourself to chicken eggs if different sorts are accessible. Eggs are rich in protein and make certain to eat the yolks, which are vitamin and fat-rich. It's not necessary to restrict yourself to unfenced or omega-3 containing eggs, but you can do as such if that accommodates your taste.

Pork

Pork is certainly allowed. Fatty cuts are liked, consider pork rib-eye, sirloin, pork steaks, and pork stomach. Pork ribs are an excellent choice but don't utilize barbecue sauce. If you need to enhance them, look for rubs and spices that are zero-carb—the more fat, the better, with the goal that you get an adequate source of energy. Pork hotdog is a great idea to include but watch for covered up carbs. Bacon and cheeks are extraordinary too.

Cooking fats

Vegetable-based cooking fats ought to stay away from. Use butter or fat for cooking. Tallow is likewise allowed.

Fish

Any fish or seafood is allowed – you can eat trout, bass, salmon, swordfish, mussels, clams, lobster, scallops, and crab. Once more, you need to abstain from going excessively far into the lean category, so while you can eat any animal from the ocean, fattier fish is liked – decide on salmon, sardines, mackerel, swordfish, and anchovies. If you're eating a leaner food like lobster, make certain to include heaps of butter and different fats; else, you'll wind up feeling hungry.

Dairy

At the point when you get into dairy you can get into a little controversy – but you ought to give a valiant effort for you. The fundamental principle is to maintain a strategic distance from carbohydrates and recall that a lot of dairy products are stacked with lactose, which is just sugar. Substantial cream can be utilized, but note that cream contains limited quantities of carbs and proteins. The measure of carbs won't be significant except if you're consuming enormous amounts like more than a cup at once. Cheese is also allowed but know about any carb content and evade low-fat assortments. If you do decide to include some milk, just choose full-fat products. Butter is certainly allowed. Remember your sensitivity circumstance. One explanation that people stay away from dairy products is it can prompt sensitivities and inflammation. Still, everybody is different, so you have to consider your circumstance as opposed to following rules another person made up. Some carnivore diet advocates stay away from dairy out and out, and strictly, dodging is in the best soul of the carnivore diet.

Protein Powders and Shakes

Meal replacements ought to be evaded on a carnivore diet. However, it is conceivable to discover whey-based (made out of milk proteins) products that are technically consistent with a carnivore diet. You may keep some protein shake blend on hand as an emergency food source to utilize if you're truly in a hurry, but different alternatives like canned meats are presumably better for this reason. If you do choose to keep some shake blends around, read the fixing list carefully and don't utilize any shake blends that contain any plant products whatsoever – so soy is certainly not allowed.

Canned Meats

Canned meats are extraordinary to have around for snacks or to give something you can eat quickly when you don't have the opportunity to cook. They are likewise extraordinary to bring for lunch to work or school. Great choices of canned meats include fish, sardines, mackerel, trout, clams, shellfish, Vienna hotdogs, anchovies, and pruned meat. Select what tastes great to you, but if you're staying away from plant foods completely, remember that many canned meats are packed in olive oil, so if you're strictly following carnivore dieting, you'll need to pick brands that are packed in water instead of fat. Unfortunately, many canned kinds of seafood are packed in unwanted vegetable oils.

Beverages

Water is it, but you should drink some bone soup also. Most completely maintain a strategic distance from caffeine and alcohol, so keep away from coffee, tea, brew, and wine. Recall that coffee is plant-based. However, utilize your judgment here. You can follow a carnivore diet and have some coffee and tea and even around zero carb alcohol products with some restraint and still keep up the soul of the diet.

Condiments, Spices, And Sauces

Salt is unquestionably allowed and certainly exhorted except if you need to eat bland meat constantly. Other people who are less strict will utilize salt and pepper, and insofar as you're going for zero-or extremely low-carb sources, you can enhance your meats with spices. Although they are generally plant-based, as a percentage of your diet, they are consumed in trace amounts, so you're not going to destroy your diet if you rub your chicken with curry or cayenne pepper. The issue here isn't calories or your insulin reaction but rather hypersensitivities and plant poisons. The best activity is to evaluate different things and perceive how they affect you and eliminate any that cause sensitivity symptoms, indigestion, or body aches. Cream-and butter-based sauces are extraordinary to include in a carnivore diet. It gives you a simple method to add fat to low-fat meats and seafood to make the meals additionally fulfilling.

Foods to avoid

The general principle for foods to keep away from on a carnivore diet is straightforward: don't eat anything plant-based. To maintain a strategic distance from:

- All fruits
- Nuts and seeds
- Oats and grain
- Wheat, grains, pasta, rice, and bread
- Condiments that are plant-based like salsa, ketchup or tartar sauce
- Olive oil, avocado oil, canola oil or any plant-based cooking oil
- Mushrooms
- Beer and wine (and alcoholic drinks by and large, since they are plant-based, but you may appreciate zero-carb assortments with some restraint)
- Sugar, nectar, and molasses
- Corn syrup, high fructose or not
- Pizza
- Agave and other exotic sugars or syrups

- Artificial sugars ought to be kept away from or utilized in strict balance.

Don't eat any foods dependent on plants or that includes fixings from plants: no ice cream and no packaged foods like crackers and cookies.

When to eat

The standard of when to eat while following a carnivore diet is basic – eat when you're ravenous. You can follow the standard example of eating three times each day, but most carnivore dieters find that it isn't necessary. Some eat one enormous meal every day, but the most common method for eating is to eat two meals per day, and you can eat them at whatever point you need. A decent guideline to attempt is to eat a large meal before anything else and another twelve hours later. Disposing of the need to go out for lunch can genuinely assist you with sticking to the diet since you won't need to bother with cafés or eating with colleagues and getting into dietary contentions and conflicts.

Common mistakes and eliminating them

The most common mix-up on the carnivore diet isn't eating enough. Since you've gone through your whole time on earth eating carbohydrates as a feature of your meal, when you move from steak and potato to steak alone, you may wind up not getting enough calories. Calorie counting isn't a piece of this diet – utilize your stomach and how you feel to control you into eating the perfect sum. If you feel powerless, tired, or you get some stomach protesting, eat more meat. A second misstep is overeating lean meats. Carbohydrates, similar to protein, give four calories for each gram while fat gives nine calories for every gram. The difference between carbohydrates and proteins, however, is the body doesn't lean toward utilizing proteins for energy and carbohydrates provide the least difficult and most easy energy source there is. Subsequently, if you eat lean cuts of meat you're not going to be fulfilled. Eating a skinless chicken bosom with rice is satisfying because the rice gives you a lot of momentary energy from its carb content. But eating a chicken bosom without anyone else – even with the skin – isn't sufficient energy. Thus, look at the cuts of meat you're selecting and consistently decide on the higher fat selection. Another common slip-up is being not able to abandon condiments. While it isn't strictly necessitated that you eliminate all sauces from your diet, they can be a source of shrouded carbohydrates and plant allergens. Become accustomed to eating a plain steak with salt and pepper – and keep away from the A1 sauce. Some may locate this exhausting from the start, but after you've done it for some time, you'll become used to eating meat without sauces. If you truly need a sauce, make an animal-based one with butter and cream that will likewise help make your meals additionally fulfilling. Another common misstep is the feeling that you can have cheat days. It is by a wide margin the best policy on a carnivore diet to abstain from having cheat days.

A cheat day may cause you to put on weight, but it is additionally going to cause you hopelessness. Once your body has acclimated to a carnivore diet, you've truly changed the bacteria in your gut. So they won't be ready to handle abrupt implantation of carbs. Subsequently, you may end up with swelling, queasiness, and stomach torments. Likewise, as we'll see below, embracing a carnivore diet implies you'll need to experience a digestive change that may include constipation or diarrhea. Having "cheat days" signifies repeated episodes of these problems as your body attempts to change. This isn't weight watchers or some other approach that includes calorie restricting the standard American diet – it's a full-scale shift of food consumption. Thus, don't play with it.

Activity: Select between 1-5 types of meat for every one of your meals for the following seven days. Create a grocery rundown of the entirety of the fixings you'll have to cook them. At that point, head to the grocery store and purchase what you need. At that point, start your carnivore diet with your next meal.

How to start cold turkey

The ideal approach to begin is to eliminate (however much as could reasonably be expected) all carbohydrates and plant-based foods from your home. Of course, if you're hitched, and your accomplice wouldn't like to go along with you on a carnivore diet, that won't be conceivable, but if you can do it, at that point dispose of each one of those food items you're not going to eat to eliminate any allurement. Donate them to a food bank or offer them to companions. To the extent your diet, the ideal approach to begin is to bounce in feet first, understanding that in the initial barely any weeks you may encounter a few issues (which we discuss below). As a major aspect of beginning with the program, go out on the town to shop and pick up the food items you'll requirement for the principal seven day stretch of the diet. And once you're committed to attempting a carnivore diet, do what needs to be done—no compelling reason to eat a meal with few vegetables first. Hop in and eat a steak and just steak for your first meal and don't look back.

Your first 30 days

Recently, psychology master, Professor Jordan Peterson, was met on the Joe Rogan podcast. They were discussing the carnivore diet, and Peterson stated: "simply attempt it for a month." This is the best advice that can be given for this diet. Attempt it for a month and simply perceive how it works out. For the initial 30 days, we accept that simplicity is your companion. Limit yourself to a few food items, so you're not contemplating what to eat and letting mental battle barge in on the process of adjusting to the diet. Therefore, we recommend being generally strict for the principal month and then expanding later, albeit some will settle on being strict over the long haul. For the main month, consider eating one to five food items. A recommended rundown of items selected for their capacity to cause you to feel satiated includes:

- Ribeye steak
- Prime rib
- New York strip steak
- Chicken thighs and wings (skin on, no BBQ sauce, the season just with salt and pepper) If you wind up craving assortment after the main week, at that point return to the allowed foods rundown and look at including more choices.

Common side effects

Some people will promptly adjust to a carnivore diet, but the vast majority will have at least one reaction. The general guideline with responses is that they are transitory as your body acclimates to another method for eating. Along these lines, one strategy is just to allow them to pass, and you should possibly stress over it if you're a month into the diet and as yet experiencing problems.

But how about we look at specific reactions that will come upon a carnivore diet.

Constipation

Constipation is the main complaint of the carnivore dieter. However, understand that you may appear to be constipated without actually being constipated. This is because the meat is all the more completely digested and consumed by the body than plant foods are. Plant foods contain a ton of undigestible substances like cellulose. Dietary fiber includes alleged "mass" to the stool, which implies you'll produce more and go all the more regularly to get the stuff out of your body you can't digest. So, if you get yourself not having bowel movements by any means, you can attempt these strategies all together:

- Drink more water. Water helps keep bowel movements moving naturally.
- Get a magnesium citrate supplement. Magnesium is an old diuretic, and

supplementing with magnesium citrate can frequently solve the problem.

- If you are as yet having problems, consider a zero-calorie fiber supplement like Metamucil. Recall that you're going to have less regular bowel movements. A few people will discover they just go every 2 or 3 days, but they are not constipated. Evaluate your circumstance given that.

Fatigue

Fatigue is a prevalent complaint with a carnivore diet and with keto diets also. The bottom line, right now, that, for as long as you can remember, your body has been depending on starches and sugars for its energy, and when you completely cut those out of your diet, at that point, it will require some investment to modify. Your body will take a stab at continuing its carb addiction by depending on the liver's stockpile of glycogen. This will quickly run out, however. Once your body adjusts by going into ketosis, exhaustion will begin to pass. In this way, the primary concern here is to release time essentially. A few people, however, experience weariness for another explanation – they just aren't eating enough food. If you are experiencing weariness, consider eating more meat (and, once more, choose fattier cuts of meat for the energy content).

Diarrhea

Many people get diarrhea while receiving a carnivore diet. There are two fundamental purposes for this:

- Water assimilation in the colon.
- Digestion of fats.

If you've been consuming a standard American diet, you've been consuming a lot of plant fiber. Fiber assists with absorbing water in your colon. At the point when you out of nowhere expel it from the diet, there is nothing to ingest that water – except the colon itself. The colon needs to figure out how to retain more water than it had been during the digestion process. This requires some serious energy, and numerous cases of diarrhea associated with a carnivore diet can be solved by essentially sticking to the diet and allowing time to pass. A few people will have problems digesting fat. If you're out of nowhere moving to a high-fat diet (moderately), at that point, your liver may not produce enough bile to digest fats appropriately. This is an issue, especially for people who've had nerve bladder problems or had their gallbladder expelled. Right now, a brief period, back off to leaner meats. At that point, step by step increase the measure of fat consumed with each meal. Diarrhea will step by step leave.

Palpitations and muscle cramps

Much of the time, heart palpitations and muscle cramps that emerge when following a carnivore diet are because of a mineral deficiency. The two minerals that lead to these problems are potassium and magnesium, albeit salt can be included too. Especially if you are having heart palpitations, a magnesium supplement of 250-500 mg for each day can be useful. It likewise reduces muscle cramps. For potassium, to increase your potassium consumption consider utilizing a "salt substitute" for a portion of your flavoring needs. These products use potassium chloride as opposed to sodium chloride. Flavoring your meat with salt to taste is typically enough to get enough salt in your diet, however, including a day by day drink of bone soup can help with salt and potassium. Pink Himalayan salt is the most ideal, and you can even place it in your water.

Meat flu

Meat flu is related to ketosis. The straightforward entry of time cures this problem as long as you strictly follow the diet.

Mental fog (early on)

Mental haze when first beginning the diet is natural and universal; like "meat flu," it's principally related to acclimation to ketosis, but it can likewise be connected to an inability to consume enough calories. If you wind up experiencing mental haze, at that point, eat and increase the measure of fatty meat you are eating for the most part.

Activity: The more you set you up the mind for this better approach for eating, the simpler it will be for you to submerge yourself into the lifestyle. But a few people just can't bounce into these sorts of things. If you don't figure you can go cold turkey immediately, simply attempt to begin with two days every week. At that point following a month or somewhere in the vicinity, attempt three days. Continue to include an ever-increasing number of meals that are completely carnivore consistently. By bit by bit advancing, it might be simpler to begin. Simply don't backtrack once you include a day!

Advanced techniques

When you find a good pace, you ought to have begun your carnivore diet if you've decided that it's something you'd prefer to attempt. Right now, going to go past just saying 'eat meat' and consider some further developed techniques that can assist you with remaining in balance and lose much more weight.

Incorporating bone broth

Bone soup is made basically from the bones of chicken or meat. Connective tissues can likewise be utilized, such as hooves, feet, and knuckles. Bone soup can likewise be produced using fish and the bones of different animals. To set it up, you boil the bones and connective tissues and then stew them for an extensive stretch (a few hours and even conceivably over a day). Salt and spices are included to enhance. Bone stock is promptly accessible nowadays in many stores, so it isn't necessary to make it yourself although you can if wanted since it is really easy to make. For what reason would you need to make and consume bone soup? The explanation is the bones of animals are packed with significant minerals and amino acids. This is significant for carnivore dieters, especially since you're not going to get as much of different minerals as your plant consuming companions are getting. Bone soup can enable you to get:

- Sodium
- Calcium
- Magnesium
- Potassium
- Phosphorous
- Zinc
- Manganese
- Copper
- Boron
- Iodine (fish-based bone soup just)

As bone stock extracts numerous substances from the bone marrow, it will likewise give some iron content, and various vitamins, including vitamin A, all the B vitamins, vitamin C, and vitamins D and K. A significant side note is that vitamin K2, which is discovered uniquely from animal sources, may help keep your veins clear by reducing calcification. In the past chapter, we noticed that some new carnivore dieters might experience muscle cramps and heart palpitations. Drinking a day by day cup of bone soup is a straightforward method to manage those sorts of problems by recharging your body with significant minerals. Bone soup likewise gives collagen. The measure of collagen in the soup is directly corresponding to the time the stock is cooked. So the more you stew the stock, the more collagen it will contain. Bone juices are different than typical juices or stock in that it's been stewed for a much longer timeframe, and so has progressively mineral and collagen content.

Applying probiotics

If you're having digestive problems while adjusting to the carnivore diet, the utilization of good probiotics can help. Your digestion relies upon bacteria in your gut which helps digest the food and move it along. The sorts of bacteria in your gut get selected for by your diet, and they become acclimated to what you're eating. If you've spent a lifetime eating half or a greater amount of your diet from carbohydrates, at that point the bacteria in your gut will be in for a shock when you go to a diet-dependent on animal products. Probiotics are products that will help your digestion because they are comprised of live bacteria and yeast for this reason. They contain purported "great bacteria." We typically consider bacteria something that causes disease, but numerous bacteria aid the basic functioning of your digestive system. The correct probiotics can help reduce diarrhea and problems like irritable bowel syndrome. The best probiotics you can get are those that are refrigerated. A dry probiotic that is sold in a significant grocery chain or huge box store is most likely going to be less effective. It may have sat away, in transport, or the store for such a long time that a great deal of the bacteria has ceased to exist. Thus, visit a local health food or vitamin store and see what refrigerated choices they have. Probiotics help renew the bacteria in your gut and can change the cosmetics of the populace. There are a couple of significant sorts you will typically discover:

- Lactobacillus: Can help with reducing diarrhea.

- Bifidobacterium: This is typically included to reduce peevish bowel syndrome.
- Bacillus coagulans: Another sort of bacteria that reduces diarrhea.
- Streptococcus thermophilus: Although the name Strep conjures up im-times of throat infections, this strain is not a disease-causing organism and assists with legitimate digestion you're experiencing diarrhea when attempting to change by a carnivore diet and you're not seeing an improvement of symptoms after some time, at that point you may profit by a probiotic. Some things to look for in selecting your probiotic are:
- Choose one that has different strains of bacteria. Some health specialists recommend, at any rate, ten different strains.
- If you can't locate a refrigerated probiotic, look for one rated to be "rack stable."
- Check the CFUs recorded on the jug. This gives you a thought of the number of live

cultures per serving. A probiotic with 50 billion CFUs is adored

CHAPTER FIVE: WHAT IS INTERMITTENT FASTING?

It's the strategic approach to eating and not eating for differing amounts of time. The topic of fasting may put a few people off, giving them dreams of a master covering up in the mountains, not eating for a considerable length of time. However, recent advancements have indicated that brief fasting can have significant health benefits. There is a wide range of ways you can incorporate fasting into a carnivore diet. If you're doing the diet right – which means eating until you're genuinely satiated – fasting will be anything but difficult to incorporate into your lifestyle. The best news is that few unobtrusive methods for doing discontinuous fasting have been created in recent years, making it simple to select the technique that works for you. Fasting has numerous advantages that can enhance those you get from following a carnivore diet. Some of the benefits attributed to intermittent fasting include:

- Lower fasting blood sugars.
- Increased insulin affectability (or said another way, decreased insulin resistance).
- Reductions in fasting triglycerides and blood pressure.
- Additional weight loss.
- Reduction in type 2 diabetes, potentially reducing the requirement for medications.

Fasting may not be for everybody. If you have a genuine medical condition if it's not too much trouble consult with a doctor before incorporating fasting into your lifestyle. The explanation fasting helps is that it works in a similar way that a keto or carnivore diet works. That is the point at which you're fasting your body goes into ketosis. If you're following a carnivore diet and have done it for any period, you're as of now in ketosis. Still, fasting allows your body to recuperate itself and use ketones for energy without taking in extra calories.

Recollect that your body has glycogen stores in your liver that can be utilized for energy by the body. At the point when you start on a carnivore diet, you'll quickly go through those glycogen stores. They can give enough energy to a brief timeframe, around a day or somewhere in the vicinity. Still, from that point forward, your body adjusts to utilizing ketosis and burning your body fat for energy. The hormone insulin assumes a central job in digestion and energy use by the body. Each time you eat, insulin is discharged in the bloodstream. At the point when you're eating carbohydrates, insulin advises the cells of the body to take up the blood sugar that enters your bloodstream when your food is digested. Insulin likewise triggers your liver to store some glucose as glycogen. However, the liver just has a limited capacity to store glycogen, and when that has been reached, the liver starts transforming glucose into fat. Some fat is put away in the liver, but its vast majority will be discharged in the bloodstream and winds up as body fat. Eating a carnivore diet encourages you in one significant manner since you're not consuming sugar; your pancreas is going to discharge less insulin when you digest your meals. To get the energy, you will need to burn off the body fat you have and make ketones out of the fat you're consuming. By fasting, you're forcing the body to utilize body fat for energy since there are no incoming calories of any sort. You don't need to go days without food to get the advantages of fasting. How about we look at a portion of the different ways that you can incorporate intermittent fasting into your diet.

Kinds of intermittent fasting

You can fast as meager or as much as you can imagine sensibly speaking. Everybody as of now fasts a smidgen. You may have supper at 6 or 7 PM each night, and you presumably don't eat again until 12 hours later (well ideally, you're not the sort of individual who is sneaking in noon snacks). That is the reason the morning meal is called breakfast; it's the merger of two words – break and fast, so it truly intends to break or end fast. The least difficult approach to incorporate fasting is to broaden the period you hang tight for "breakfast."

Fasting

As noted above, numerous people effectively "fast" by holding up 10-12 hours between their last meal of the day (supper) and their first meal of the following day (breakfast). A few people even skip breakfast. On a carb-loaded diet, that is not a smart thought, but if you're following a keto or carnivore lifestyle, it can be useful. The 16/8 technique for fasting is exceptionally simple to follow. What you can do is to take part right now fasting is to compress the time range inside which you eat to an eight-hour term. You can do this any way you need, and it very well may be done a couple of days seven days, or day by day, whatever works best for you. A few alternatives could be:

- Eat supper at 5 PM, at that point don't eat again until 9 AM the following day.

- Skip breakfast altogether. Eat around early afternoon, and then have supper at 7-8 PM. Since a carnivore meal is more fulfilling and enduring than one dependent on carbohydrates, which give energy that dissipates quickly, fasting right now simple to incorporate. Numerous people on a carnivore diet quickly gravitate to just eating twice every day. In this way, they can wind up doing a 16/8 strategy for intermittent fasting without considering it.

Day by day 23-hour fasting

A few people on a carnivore diet get by just eating once every day. You can attempt this by eating an extremely hearty meal until you're entirely satiated. You may think about this as a chasm and fast technique. Some accept this might be the way that numerous prehistoric tracker gatherers ate their meals. They were not in a position where they could plan out three little meals for each day and go to the fridge to get put away food. They ate when they had food and didn't eat again until they found or killed something. This technique won't work for each one, but it's something you can attempt to check whether it works for you. Eating once every day is otherwise called the "warrior diet."

5/2 fasting

Eating just once a day can be expanded into having a couple of days out of each week when you don't eat by any stretch of the imagination. This technique is commonly called 5/2 fasting. Utilizing this approach, you fast two days per week and eat the other five days ordinarily. There are even different ways you can execute a 5/2 fast:

- On your fasting days, just beverage water and consume no food by any means.
- Alternatively, for an increasingly unobtrusive approach on your fasting days despite everything consume food, but in an exceptionally constrained sum – state 500 calories.

- So-called alternate day fasting – adopts the strategy of eating negligible calories (500 every day) up a notch. You eat 500 calories in a day, at that point eat typical calories the following, and then rehash.
- You can likewise attempt 6/1 fasting, that is, eating typically six days per week and fasting one day of the week. Over two days of fasting for each week isn't advised, in any event for a great many people.

Occasional fasting

It's not necessary to incorporate constant fasting into your diet to get the advantages. You can likewise have a one day fast periodically. This could be done once per week, once at regular intervals, or even just once every month.

Impact of intermittent fasting on insulin sensitivity and blood sugar

Intermittent fasting – by blowing through your glycogen stores and forcing your body into ketosis, burning your body fat in the process – is exceptionally beneficial for keeping up healthy blood sugar and increasing insulin affectability. If you're not consuming any calories, the measure of insulin in your bloodstream is going to drop significantly. This assists people with balancing out their blood sugars. Such a reset can be useful for people with metabolic syndrome and prediabetes. Fasting, incorporated with a carnivore diet, may assist some with peopling reverse these kinds of metabolic disorders; Fasting likewise assists with metabolic problems indirectly. Health issues related to blood sugar are regularly directly caused by or related to your body weight. Since fasting will assist speed with weighting loss, it will help fix defective metabolism. Triglycerides regularly move in sync with blood sugars. That is, people with high fasting blood sugars and high A1C values additionally will, in general, have high triglycerides. Recall that triglycerides are a significant heart attack risk, and eating a high-carbohydrate diet (or consuming an excessive amount of alcohol) are significant risk factors with regards to high triglycerides. Fasting has been appeared to reduce triglycerides. Along these lines, by incorporating fasting into your carnivore diet, you'll accelerate the process to improved health by fixing blood sugar and triglyceride problems. The risk of type 2 diabetes can be significantly reduced, and some claim that type 2 diabetics can even be cured with this approach.

Autophagy

Autophagy intends to eat yourself. Try not to let that scare you; however, in the human body, the process of autophagy is progressively similar to clearing out garbage. That isn't required (and possibly destructive). Fasting triggers autophagy, which places the body in a healthier state. This happens because the resistant system will be activated to clean out (demolish) old and dysfunctional cells all through the body. Your body is continually utilizing some level of autophagy, but the level of autophagy is significantly increased by fasting. The scientific subtleties aren't generally significant. You can necessarily consider autophagy cleaning out and disposing of all the garbage. Envision your front yard brimming with garbage like junk and old rusted out and stalled cars. Autophagy would be what could be compared to pulling all the garbage away and planting new grass and trees, so your yard is nice and healthy once more. Stressful circumstances in particular, starvation – trigger a significant increase in autophagy. You may consider it the body's method for modifying itself to with-stand the stressful circumstance. Fasting, which is exceptionally momentary starvation, helps increase autophagy. It is associated with ketosis, so by following a carnivore type diet, you're most likely previously setting off an increased level of autophagy. Since it clears out old and harmed merchandise from your body, autophagy slows down the maturing process. Fasting and reduced calorie consumption have been appeared to increase lifespan in animal models, and it's accepted this works for humans also. The uplifting news for carnivore dieters is that if you're eating a lot of carbohydrates in your diet, at that point significantly reduced calories are expected to appreciate the advantages. With a keto or carnivore diet, when you're getting a great deal or the greater part of your energy from fat constantly, you can get the advantages without lessening calorie consumption on non-fasting days. In fact, if you follow the warrior diet or utilize 16/8 fasting, you don't need to reduce generally speaking calorie consumption by any stretch of the imagination.

Benefits of intermittent fasting

Intermittent fasting can likewise prompt increased development hormones and lower blood pressure. If it's handled carefully, it can likewise improve body composition by decreasing body fat without losing muscle mass. For this to occur, ensure you're getting a decent measure of protein when not fasting. This isn't re-partner an issue if you're following a carnivore diet.

Must I fast?

Intermittent fasting can be thought of like the icing on the cake. It will help magnify the advantages of a carnivore diet, but it's not necessary to include fasting to get the benefits of a carnivore lifestyle. If adding fasting to your lifestyle offers to you, give it a shot and perceive how it works. You may have a go at sliding into fasting by beginning with a 16/8 technique and working toward 6/1 and then 5/2 fasting. Make sure to consult your doctor before beginning an intermittent fasting program consistently. This standard applies to type 2 diabetics, in particular, especially if you're on insulin.

Activity: Go to your local health food mall and select decent bone juices and probiotics to incorporate into your carnivore lifestyle.

Exercise and Workouts

If you're considering a carnivore diet, you're most likely very health conscious. In this way, you're most likely previously doing a type of exercise schedule. But remember that exercise isn't necessary to get more fit while on a carnivore diet – removing carbs from your diet will deal with that practically automatically. The greatest issue with regards to exercise and the carnivore diet is that, at first, you may have energy problems.

Working out while on carnivore diet

When beginning with a carnivore diet, it's prudent to limit the time and exertion spent working out during the principal week. You have to let your body conform to having not many or zero carbs – this is a dramatic shift. However, it is essential to disperse the common fantasy that a lot of carbs are necessary to perform well athletically. It's been indicated this isn't the case – the body can perform very well on a ketogenic or carnivore diet with regards to exercise and athletic activity. While it's anecdotal, carnivore fan Shawn Baker has increased his athletic performance while on a carnivore diet. He can deadlift 700 pounds and is a top-level competitor in indoor paddling. One explanation that carbs are considered fundamental is that glycogen or put away starch is kept in the muscles for physical activity. It's essential to acknowledge, however, that glycogen stores will be kept up at a natural level by your body. We've recently noticed that protein can be made into glucose by the body if it needs it. However, adjustment to the carnivore diet is something any practitioner needs to experience. Much the same as your digestive system needs to adjust; your muscles should adapt also. It's commonly accepted that you will see a few declines in performance when beginning the carnivore diet, but that these will improve after some time. While there aren't numerous hard information on the subject yet, anecdotal reports indicate that around three weeks to a month are necessary to return to top performance. Aerobic activity will endure more than weightlifting or resistance preparation. But, after some time, both should come back to ordinary as your body adjusts.

Pitfalls of working out

The most significant entanglement of working out when following a carnivore lifestyle doesn't have enough energy. If you're experiencing difficulty getting into your workouts, add more food to your diet. While including increasingly fat can help with the energy, you have to likewise focus on including more protein. If you're doing cardio and quality preparing, you'll have to up your food consumption significantly more.

Cardio

Take the first month of your carnivore diet to allow the body to adjust. You ought to abbreviate the time spent doing cardio during the underlying periods of the diet. There are no immovable principles; you have to test and see what your body can handle, but a decent general guideline is, to begin with, 10 minutes of exercise and slowly increase. This may cause a few people tension, but recollect, this is just transitory. In this way, you'll go through seven days, completing 10 minutes of exercise, at that point, add 5-10 minutes to your schedule the following week. As your body becomes changed by ketosis, you'll discover your workouts start to come simpler. A few people will even end up performing at a higher level. If you end up truly having problems, look toward increasing your food consumption. Do it a smidgen at once, beginning by including a couple of eggs (white and yolk) or a little increase in the measure of meat at your meals. The sort of cardio you include in your routine is up to you. Scientists have discovered that low-level and low-impact cardio is the most beneficial with regards to advancing health and reducing the risk of heart attack and stroke. This is because low-level exercise reduces inflammation, which is the significant cause of heart disease when you get directly down to it. Great low-impact exercise schedules include:

- Walking, at any rate, 30 minutes out of every day five times each week.
- Running at a slow pace (running). Scientists have discovered that running only 5 minutes of the day produces the

most advantage, but 20-minute meetings 3-5 times each week are advised.

- Swimming, if you approach. Swimming is an excellent choice for exercise because it doesn't stress the joints. Focus on 20 brief meetings around 3-5 times each week.
- Bicycling can be an excellent type of exercise, and like running, it very well may be made as light or severe as wanted. A 20 brief bicycle ride for every day is sufficient for significant health benefits. Those progressively inspired by exceptional work-outs and pinnacle wellness can go for long rides of 2 hours or more, or you can consider additionally challenging rides like mountain biking if you live close to a region where that is a choice.
- Hitting the gym is a possibility for those who'd incline toward doing that instead of exercising outside; you can utilize stationary bicycles and treadmills to get a large number of similar advantages.

Yoga

Yoga is an incredible method for exercising that can help in various regions. It's especially useful for carnivore dieters because it won't be as impacted by the change stage as traditional cardio will be. Advantages cited from yoga include:

- Stress reduction and an improved feeling of health.
- Reduced inflammation.
- Increased flexibility.
- Improved tone and balance.
- Better resistance to injury while taking part in other physical activities.
- Better metabolism and more balance.

Resistance Training

Like different types of exercise, resistance, and quality training are tormented by the fantasy that you have to consume a lot of carbs to get results. This essentially isn't valid, and a quick search on the web uncovers that some well-muscled competitors are practitioners of the carnivore or ketogenic diet. The primary issues with resistance training on the carnivore diet rotate on having enough energy, adjustment, and getting enough protein. Likewise, with any type of physical activity, the body will experience an adjustment stage as the body becomes acclimated to getting by without consuming carbohydrates. During this step, you may find that your workouts are increasingly difficult. Remember that the more athletic and performance situated you are, the more you'll be faced with these problems. Most by far of people are doing whatever it takes not to enter an athletic competition, however, and so the problem of adjustment will be minor. And in all cases, the body will adjust to the new diet, and so everybody will overcome this challenge, which is, for the most part, a short time. It can, likewise, involve not eating enough. Start by giving yourself a baseline. Discover the amount you have to eat to just get past the day without doing exercise. At that point, on days, you have substantial workouts, increase your food consumption. If you are doing quality training and feel that you can't perform or include muscle, add more protein to your diet. You ought to do this without utilizing supplements except if it's essential. Including eggs, canned meats like fish, or more steak is the favored approach. If you wind up needing to utilize a supplement, use whey protein, and don't use plant-based alternatives like soy. A resistance training routine can utilize hand weights or free weights or a combination of both, or if accessible, you can use machines. Weight machines can help fabricate quality and muscle, but using free weights will help improve your balance also. As a rule, free weights produce more outcomes, but what kind and the level of results wanted fluctuates from individual to individual. Your workout should look for a balance between the upper and lower body and at-entice to focus on all muscle groups. If you are endeavoring to increase your performance, routinely adding to the weight utilized for each exercise is a significant component of your training. You can accomplish this by adding 3-5 pounds to the weight used each week or two. Activities that can be included in your routine include:

- Bench press: for the most part to exercise the chest zone. If you're new to quality training and not utilizing a machine, make sure to have an accomplice spot you in case the weight you're using becomes an excessive amount to handle.
- Military press: this includes lifting a weight from shoulder level over your head. Fundamentally builds shoulder quality.
- Pull-downs: fundamentally to manufacture upper back or lat muscles Requires a machine.
- Bent over lines: you can utilize this with either free weights or hand weights as an alternative to pull-downs.
- Arm curls: build bicep muscles and, to a lesser degree, lower arm quality. You can do arm curls in a variety of approaches to challenge your muscles differently and to create different muscles in conjunction

with your biceps. For instance, you can do sitting one arm curls or standing two arm curls, and if accessible, isolate the biceps utilizing an incline.

- Leg curls and leg augmentations to construct thigh and hamstring muscles.
- Calf raises to assemble calf muscles.
- Deadlifts: assists work with coring quality.
- Squats: for leg quality. Remember that it very well may be difficult for the knees and even cause genuine injury. It's not necessary to do all workouts recorded here; select a subset of workouts that gets your legs, shoulders, biceps, and chest. For each exercise, start with three arrangements of 10 reps, done 2-3 times each week. If you are a novice to weight lifting, start slowly, and develop your direction. Getting on edge when beginning a weightlifting program is counter-productive, as you'll end up sore and stiff and conceivably reluctant to continue with an exercise program. If you need to work out at home,

some low-cost and capable weight benches are accessible that even include pulleys and other extra hardware, empowering you to do exercises like lat pull-downs and leg curls.

Activity: If you're not currently incorporating an exercise routine into your health plan, select an aerobic exercise to complete three times each week for at any rate 30 minutes for each meeting and start quality training by doing bodyweight exercises.

CHAPTER SIX: MAKING A MEAL PLAN

At the point when you start the diet, it assists with having a meal plan in place, so you don't need to over-think what you will do each time you are eager. The meal plans you start with may not be one you stick to the long haul, but the key is to begin, and then you can make the necessary changes so your meals will better accommodate your lifestyle and tastes. When you create your meal plan, ensure that you incorporate a decent arrangement of variety in it, especially during the initial ten days. You may begin preferring steak, but if you are eating it consistently, you may before long feel worn out on it and will tumble off the wagon.

The motivation behind having a meal plan is to help facilitate your change without the additional stress of not recognizing what to cook or eat. Below are a couple of recommendations to kick you off. We start with food choices for one day on the strict carnivore diet, where it is simply meat. A 4-day guide follows this to progressively adaptable carnivore eating, where you can change it up.

STRICT DIET

Breakfast

5 bacon slices

(You may likewise choose to skip breakfast and fast until lunch if you are incorporating intermittent fasting, which we will come to soon).

Lunch

Rib-eye steak, or chicken livers, seasoned with salt and pepper.

Snack

1 cup bone juices

Supper

Three cheeseburger patties seasoned with cayenne, onion powder, garlic powder, salt, and pepper, or two huge salmon filets.

LOOSER DIET

Day 1:

Breakfast: 3 eggs cooked in organic butter from grass-took care of cows

4 slices of bacon

2 slices of cheese

1 cup of black coffee or tea

Lunch: ½ lb. ground hamburger arranged with ½ cup of cheese

Supper: 12 oz. steak arranged with organic butter

–

Day 2:

Breakfast: Ham and Omelet

Lunch: 1 chicken bosom cooked with a ½ cup of parmesan cheese 2 slices of bacon 1 cup of bone stock.

Supper: Classic Roast Chicken

Day 3:

Breakfast: Pork Sausage and Eggs

Lunch: 12 oz. steak arranged with organic butter.

Supper: Two fish filets (tilapia, catfish, red snapper) 1 cup of bone stock 2 slices of cheese –

Day 4:
Breakfast: Same as Day 1

Lunch: ½ lb. ground turkey cooked with ½ cup of parmesan cheese

Supper: Basic Baked Salmon

As should be obvious, the meals are truly basic and easy to cook, but since you will be cooking a large portion of them yourself, it is as yet significant that you have them planned out well early. At long last, a couple of extra tips to support you.

- Plan for snacks between meals. You may not require them but carry around a touch of cheese or jerky just in case you get a craving for something before the following meal.
- Remember, your objective is zero carbs, so whenever you have a craving for carbs (for the most part occurs toward the start of the diet), substitute the carbs for fat.
- Avoid lean meats and pick fattier cuts for more satiation.

Remember that once you begin, your body is going to locate its mood. As it does, you may find that you are not inclined to eat each of the three meals in the day. Try not to force-feed yourself. If you are not ravenous, don't eat. It is as straightforward as that. Work in agreement with your body, not against it.

Friends, family and eating tut

While you might be excited about leaving on the carnivore diet, don't expect that people around you are going to share your energy. The carnivore diet is moderately new and considered radical by numerous people who don't know about its multiple advantages. In this way, it is significant not to be pushy with friends and family with the diet.

Introducing carnivorous diet to your family

With regard to food and dieting, you may help yourself out and consider it a strict issue. Much the same as people don't care for their relatives who've recently discovered God pushing their convictions on every other person, people won't be exceptionally enthusiastic about you promoting an extreme diet on them. Indeed, we are utilizing the word outrageous, but right now, calling the carnivore diet extraordinary not in the sense that it may have a pessimistic impact on your health but rather by just taking note of it excludes a few significant food groups that people are accustomed to eating every day. Likewise, recall that, for quite a long time, the medical and nutritional foundations have been caught up with pushing the idea that fat and meat is awful for you when consumed in significant amounts. All the people around you have been subject to this brainwashing their whole lives, and numerous people are not keen on surrendering their preferred foods – which may include bread and sugary items regardless of whether it isn't in their best health interests. Since the carnivore diet is such a significant change, out of nowhere, pushing it on people is going to cause numerous to feel irritated. People are additionally going to consider it to be a significant health risk. Recall that they've been convinced that they are going to drop dead if they neglect to consume the "prescribed" quantity of fruits and vegetables every day or get enough entire grains. Likewise, recollect that they haven't yet made the connection between their body aches and pains, stomach torment, and acid reflux with plant foods that you have. Indeed, even the keto diet is considered outrageous by generally, although it is experiencing a massive increase in prominence. Since the carnivore diet is the keto diet made a few strides further, a great many people who haven't heard anything about it are going to see it with suspicion. Something else to consider is that receiving meat just diet is generally simple to incorporate with everyone around you. Except if you're hitched to a veggie lover or routinely eating at vegetarian just cafés, getting meat is the least of your problems. Along these lines, you can eat with loved ones and let them eat whatever they need while you just have the meat. As a rule, this won't cause issues; of course, if they are slathering on the sugar-loaded barbecue sauce, there may be a problem, but just casually let your friends realize you'd incline toward your cuts without the sauce. If you proceed right now, you can proceed with your carnivore diet without being a weight on any other individual or coming across as a pushy aggressor. What is one of the most exceedingly awful things you can consider about vegans? It's generally that they are passionate about their diet and demand every other person follow it. They most likely accept they are sparing the planet. If you consider a vegetarian pushing their diet and plan on you as a meat eater and what they look like down their nose at you, at that point, you'll start to have an appreciation for how you may cause others to feel if you attempt to push carnivore dieting on them. It's ideal to when in doubt, refrain from interfering.

You set the example

If you're overweight or diabetic, the carnivore diet is going to impact you in a major manner. You're going to quickly get in shape, look better, and feel much improved, and after your body adjusts to the carnivore diet, you will have significantly more energy. After some time, your general health will increase, and you'll improve numbers from your doctor. Your body aches and joint pain may vanish, and your physical wellness will increase.

This will represent itself with no issue. After people move beyond the "well father is somewhat bizarre, just eating steaks," they'll begin feeling that possibly there is something to this. If you drop a few pounds per month and begin bouncing off the dividers with energy, it will be difficult to disregard. In this way, don't force the diet on anybody; follow it, and let people see the advantages for themselves. There is nothing right now is more convincing than that.

Family congruent meals (paleo or keto)

One path forward with family is having them adjust to a less demanding and restrictive diet plan. Prior, we investigated transitioning between carnivore and paleo or keto. This is conceivable because paleo and keto can be seen as checkpoints while in transit to a carnivore diet since they are both dependent on taking out different plant-based food groups that cause health issues. A decent initial step to bring your family along on a carnivore diet is to investigate paleo meals. This effectively lets your family have a meat-centered diet with you but allowing them to eat fruits and vegetables that they need. Alternatively, the keto diet will be a far simpler sell than a hard and fast carnivore diet. It's additionally simpler to get everybody on the same wavelength if the family is eating keto while you're following a carnivore diet. At last, however, understand that much of the time, having relatives do something besides what they need is perfectly workable. You can simply eat the meat out of each meal while they make the most of their potatoes. If any of your relatives are having health issues related to plant consumption, however, discussing choices like the keto or carnivore diet might be increasingly appropriate.

Carnivore and kids

This issue will impact children all things considered, from newborn children to youngsters. No research has been done on this, so no health or medical advice cannot be offered concerning whether a carnivore diet is positive or negative for children. However, it's realized that eating meat is perfectly fine, so kids of any age can certainly appreciate meat as a component of their diets. Allows first to consider taking care of newborn children and little children. Breastfeeding is completely natural, so little children can likewise consume milk without problems. However, once they get into the phase of starting to eat strong foods, meat can be introduced. It's been advised that little children need a ton of iron in their diets, so red meat ought to be incorporated. All out carnivore most likely isn't fitting; you should presumably likewise incorporate vegetables. Eggs are an excellent expansion to the diet of little children. Once more, however, it's essentially not they are known whether a carnivore diet is healthy for children or not since no research has been finished. Along these lines, now, it's most likely best not to put little children on a carnivore diet, but you can incorporate meat, which has been done since the very beginning. As a rule, being liberal in your approach to your children's diets is prudent. You would prefer not to meddle with their social circumstances with strict dietary constraints, so you ought to presumably allow them to appreciate cake and ice cream or pizza when going to parties. As children get more seasoned and get into their high school years, they are going to start having free wants and their thoughts about what they ought to eat.

Cheat days and meals

A cheat day won't ruin your life, but as a rule, cheat days ought to be evaded. And no more, you ought to have cheat days on a once in some time premise, at most once every month. The problem with a cheat day is two-overlap – it will remove your body from ketosis. This is anything but an immense issue, however, because you'll go directly back into ketosis when you continue carnivore dieting. The second problem, however, is you'll encourage an arrival to digestive problems, and you may have issues returning to carnivore dieting. After adjusting ing to the carnivore diet once, you're most likely not going to be keen on experiencing that on different occasions.

Social gatherings

Social get-togethers can be an issue, and it may be the place you'll need to incorporate a cheat day. For instance, you may need to go to a wedding, and you're basically on the snare for eating what they give at the reception. People may look at you bizarre if you do not eat a piece of cake, but nowadays, "I'm on a tight eating routine" is an answer generally comprehended by a great many people. Since we live in a meat-based society, typical meals will include meat, so it will be conceivable just to eat meat and evade other food items. You can skip treat, or you can even give yourself consent to have a cheat day for the special occasion being referred to – realizing that you should live with the consequences and committing to the genuine work that will be required to recover from it. With regards to drinks, stick to water, or soft drink water.

What to do if you slip up

Missteps on diets are inescapable. On the carnivore diet, since it's very straightforward in concept and usage, there truly aren't a lot of missteps you can make. The main mix-up – which is very common, is essentially not eating enough. If you're discovering, you essentially need more energy after allowing for a change/adjustment stage; at that point, eat more. Investigate the cuts of meats you're also selecting. If the energy level is a problem, you may need to up your fat admission. If you wrongly eat a few carbohydrates, regardless of whether it's cake at a birthday celebration or tumbling off the wagon while eating out with friends, basically get back on the program the following day. Try not to kill yourself or beat yourself up or even waste much energy pondering it. Just come back to the carnivore diet immediately.

Activity: Arrange to manage to eat with relatives and friends; that would allow you to follow your carnivore diet without forcing it on any other person.

Carnivore recipes

Presently, how about we set up certain specifics to make following the carnivore diet a breeze. A few people incline toward the ultimate in simplicity, and on the carnivore diet, that is completely conceivable. For instance, Shawn Baker is known to eat only rib eye steaks. If that seems like something that could work out for you, at that point, you shouldn't have to mess with this chapter. You can essentially go out and purchase your steaks and begin eating them. Of course, numerous, if not a great many people will locate that somewhat exhausting, so we should investigate foods we can eat on the carnivore diet and a few recipes. The Carnivore Food list

The carnivore food list is entirely basic and can be separated into a few sections. We'll classify carnivore dieters into three classes for this reason: strict, moderate, and liberal. In all cases, just animal products will be consumed, and if you're a liberal carnivore dieter, you will eat all foods, including those on the strict and moderate rundown. Strict food list, the strict food list is basic meat items. Any are allowed, but we attempt to settle on higher fat assortments to guarantee we are getting enough energy.

- Ribeye steak
- T-bone steak
- New York strip steak
- Prime rib
- Beef back ribs (will, in general, have little meat since these are the place prime rib is cut from)
- Beef short ribs (can have a decent measure of fat-containing meat, but differs a great deal)
- Roast meat
- Flank steak
- Pork chops
- Pork Sirloin
- Pork rib eye roast
- Pork midsection
- Chicken thighs (skin on)
- Chicken wings

- Chicken legs
- Whole chicken
- Duck breasts or entire duck
- Any poultry – eat the skin with it.
- Salmon, fish, swordfish, mackerel, sardines, trout
- Any other fish but fatty fish is very much wanted, lean fish can be problematic with satiety.
- Turkey, with skin.
- Rock Cornish hens
- Eggs
- Salt and pepper for seasonings
- Pork rib eye roast

Moderate rundown include the following:

- Liver (note – contains carbohydrates as glycogen)
- Other organ meats including chicken gizzards, hamburger, and chicken heart
- Butter

- Low-carb or zero-carb spices and rubs (note plant-based, but it's an unimportant sum that won't impact the vast majority)
- Sausage (note that a few assortments may have modest quantities of carbohydrates, check carefully)

Liberal list

Include a strict and moderate rundown and can include the following:

- Heavy cream
- Full-fat cheeses
- Low-carb sauces and condiments can include mustard simply don't tell your carnivore friends.
- Lean seafood that requires an expansion of cream/butter sauces to make a fantastic meal (scallops, lobster, crab)
- Exotic meats like elk, these will, in general, be exceptionally lean and so will require an

expansion of cream/butter sauces and cheese

- Processed meats

Cheap alternatives for the carnivore diet

Not every person can stand to eat rib-eye steaks seven days per week, so you can look at low-cost choices to add to your diet.

- Canned sardines. If following a strict carnivore diet, get packed in water.
- Canned fish (again search out packed in water)
- Vienna frankfurters (very reasonable, high energy)
- Hot canines (read names – go for higher fat assortments and ensure negligibly or zero carb content)
- Lunch meats
- Chicken legs (low cost, an incredible source of fat and protein)

- Cheese sticks for those following a progressively liberal carnivore diet
- High-fat ground hamburger

Where to discover carnivore diet choices

Carnivore diet choices can be found anyplace. Simply head to your meat section. When eating out, just inquire as to whether you can get the meat thing individually.

Breakfast recipes

For breakfast, the carnivore can just broil eggs in a dish and eat without anyone else, with sautéed steak, with frank, or have the traditional bacon and eggs meal with no toast.

Rib Eye Steak and Egg Omelet No Cream/Cheese Alternate

Ingredients:

- 3 tablespoons of butter
- Salt and ground pepper

- ½ pound of sliced rib-eye (or cut of your choice)
- 6 eggs

Instructions:

1. Heat a big medium pan, with 2 tablespoons of butter.
2. Season steak with salt and pepper and add to the container—Cook for 90 seconds on each side.
3. Transfer the steak to a plate. Add one spoonful of butter to the pan.
4. Whisk the eggs in a separate dish with salt and pepper. Fill the container.
5. Cook eggs until external edges start to set. Lift external edges of egg blend and channel uncooked egg toward the center.
6. Add steak blend to the other side of the omelet.
7. Flip the untopped side of the egg over the steak. Expel from container and serve.

Carnivore Cowboy Breakfast Skillet

Ingredients:

- 3 tablespoons of butter
- Salt and ground pepper
- Breakfast meat of your choice
- 4 eggs
- 1 cup of destroyed provolone cheese (discretionary)

Instructions:

1. Preheat oven to 400 degrees.
2. Using an oven-safe skillet, crumble hotdog, and cook over medium heat.
3. Separate hotdog to make wells.
4. Crack eggs and place one egg into a well.
5. Place the skillet into the oven and prepare for 5 minutes.
6. Remove from the oven. If utilizing cheese, finish off with cheese.

Bacon-wrapped Hard-Boiled Eggs

Ingredients:

- Salt and ground pepper
- 6 slices of bacon
- 6 eggs

Instructions:

1. Hard boil your eggs. At the point when cooked, strip shells and slice each egg in half.
2. Fry your bacon in a skillet exactly as you would prefer.
3. Cut bacon slices down the middle.
4. Wrap each egg half in bacon.

Easy Bacon and Eggs

Ingredients:

- Salt and ground pepper
- 4 slices of thick-cut bacon
- 3 eggs

Instructions:

1. Heat huge pan over medium heat.
2. Add bacon and cook as wanted.
3. Remove bacon, leaving oil in the container.

4. Cook your eggs in the bacon oil, flavoring eggs with salt and pepper.
5. Remove eggs and place on a plate, pouring outstanding bacon oil onto the plate (get all the fat calories you need).

Smoked Salmon and Eggs

Ingredients:

- 1 tablespoon of butter
- Salt and ground pepper
- Package of smoked salmon
- 3 eggs

Instructions:

1. Heat a big medium pan, with 2 tablespoons of butter.
2. Cook your eggs as wanted, flavoring with salt and pepper to taste.
3. Add to plate with smoked salmon.

Heated Sausage and Egg Carnivore Sandwiches

Ingredients:

- 3 tablespoons of butter
- Salt and ground pepper
- Roll of breakfast frankfurter
- 4 eggs
- 3 tablespoons of substantial cream
- 1 cup of destroyed provolone cheese

Instructions:

1. Preheat oven to 350 degrees.
2. Slice frankfurter into 8 slices. Place 4 in the heating container.
3. Create a little edge around each slice of frankfurter.
4. Crack your eggs and place on each frankfurter slice.
5. Gently place remaining wiener slices on each egg.
6. Bake for 25-30 minutes.

T-Bone Steak and Eggs

Ingredients:

- 1 tablespoon of butter

- Salt and ground pepper
- T-bone steak
- 2-3 eggs

Instructions:

1. Heat huge skillet over medium heat, with 2 tablespoons of butter.
2. Salt and pepper steak to taste.
3. Cook steak to favored doneness.
4. Add butter and cook eggs utilizing your favored strategy.
5. Remove the eggs and serve.

Lunch Recipes

The vast majority will be faced with carrying lunch to the office or eating out. If you are eating out, basically demand a meat thing with nothing else. You can even do this at fast food outlets where they will, for the most part, be glad to accommodate you and give you just hamburger patties. If they won't, just solicitation for no ketchup and expel the patties from your burgers.

Burgers

Ingredients:

- Ground hamburger
- Salt and pepper to taste
- 1 tablespoon of butter

Instructions:

1. Melt the butter in a pan over average heat.
2. Season ground hamburger with salt and pepper. Structure into patties.
3. Fry in a container until done.

Bacon Cheeseburgers

Ingredients:

- Ground meat
- 3-4 slices of bacon
- Salt and pepper to taste
- Slices of cheese (discretionary)

Instructions:

1. Heat skillet over medium heat.

2. Cut each bacon slice into 5-6 pieces, fry in a dish.
3. Remove bacon, leave the oil in the dish.
4. Mix bacon with ground meat into patties, season to taste.
5. Fry patties in a dish until done.
6. Optionally, finish off with a slice of cheese. You can additionally include a bright side up or over-simple egg for additional calories and flavor.

Carnivore snacks

If you're doing the carnivore diet correctly, you don't have to snack. In any case, you can keep food items like processed meats, hamburger jerky (check seasonings and flavorings utilized), canned fish or Vienna frankfurters, and cheese sticks on hand for snacks. Canned mackerel and sardines are incredible snacks because of their high-fat content but check if they are packed in olive oil.

Poultry Recipes Roast Chicken

Ingredients:

- Chicken
- Salt and pepper

Instructions:

1. Preheat oven to 350 degrees.
2. Salt and pepper the chicken outwardly and inside the cavity.
3. Bake for 1 hour to 1 hour and 15 minutes.

Duck Breasts

Ingredients:

- 2 Tablespoons of butter
- Duck breasts
- Salt and pepper to taste

Instructions:

1. Preheat oven to 400 degrees.
2. Scrap the thick skin of the duck breasts by cutting perpendicular in 3-4 cuts to the longwise direction of the bosom.
3. Season on the two sides with salt and pepper.

4. Place skillet over medium-high heat and cook skin side down for about
5. 4-5 minutes.
6. Turnover and cook for an extra 2 minutes.
7. Place in heating skillet and prepare for 5-10 minutes.
8. Save the fat in the container.
9. Place duck breasts on a plate, and sprinkle with extra butter and duck fat from the container.

Chicken Wings

Ingredients:

- 8-10 chicken wings for every serving
- Salt and pepper

Instructions:

1. Preheat oven to 42
2. Season the chicken wings with pepper and salt to taste. You can likewise cut into sections if wanted, or purchase wingettes.
3. Bake for 25 minutes or until done.

Chicken Thighs

Ingredients:

- 3-4 chicken thighs, skin-on per serving
- Salt and pepper

Instructions:

1. Preheat oven to 37
2. Season your chicken thighs with pepper and salt to taste.
3. Bake for 30-40 minutes until done.
4. Pour extra chicken oil on a plate with chicken to get the additional fat calories.

Baked Chicken Quarters

Ingredients:

- Chicken quarters (legs + thighs together, now and again additionally called leg quarters)
- Salt and pepper

Instructions:

1. Preheat oven to 400 degrees.

2. Season chicken quarters to taste.
3. Bake for 35-40 minutes.

Meat recipes (Beef, lamb, pork)

Butter-treated Rib Eye Steak (Can substitute porterhouse or T-bone)

Ingredients:

- 3 tablespoons of butter
- Ribeye steaks
- 1 teaspoon each of salt and pepper

Instructions:

1. Melt butter.
2. Heat pan on medium to medium-high.
3. Salt and pepper your steaks to taste, at that point, treat with dissolved butter.
4. Cook steaks in pan around 5-9 minutes to the desired doneness.

New York Strip Steak

Ingredients:

- 3 tablespoons of butter

- 2 8-ounce New York strip steaks (don't trim)
- 1 teaspoon each of salt and pepper

Instructions:

1. Melt butter.
2. Heat pan on medium-high.
3. Cook steaks in pan around 8-9 minutes to the desired doneness.
4. Place steaks on slicing board and slice into even cuts. Sprinkle with more butter.

Singed Beef Heart

Ingredients:

- Tablespoon of butter or grease
- 4 slices of hamburger heart
- Salt and pepper to taste

Instructions:

1. Cut heart slices about an inch thick eat.
2. Heat a skillet with butter on high for around 45 seconds.

3. Place heart slices in the skillet. The temperature ought to be sufficiently high to sizzle.
4. Cook to medium uncommon, around 5 minutes for each side.
5. Drizzle with dissolved butter.
6. For those utilizing cream, heat 2/3 cup of cream with a tablespoon of butter to a boil, at that point shower over your hamburger heart slices.

Lamb Chops

Ingredients:

- 2 tablespoons of butter
- Rack of lamb, cut into 4 chops.
- Salt and pepper to taste

Instructions:

1. Melt butter in a pan over average heat.
2. Season lamb chops with salt and pepper.
3. Fry in pan around 4-5 minutes for every side, contingent upon the ideal doneness.

Pork Rib Eye Roast

Ingredients:

- Salt and pepper to taste
- Pork rib eye roast

Instructions:

1. Preheat oven to 350 degrees.
2. Season roast by scouring salt and pepper outwardly.
3. Bake for 60 minutes (relies upon the weight of your roast) until inside reaches a temperature of 145 degrees.

Seafood Easy broiled salmon or trout

(Also consider arctic char)

Ingredients:

- 4-ounce salmon filets
- Salt and pepper

Instructions:

1. Preheat your broiler.
2. Season salmon filets to taste.

3. Place the skin side down on the heating sheet.
4. Broil for 8-10 minutes until cooked through.

Creamed Scallops

(Can likewise substitute lobster or crab, cook appropriately)

Ingredients:

- Scallops
- Salt and pepper
- Heavy cream
- 4 tablespoons of butter

Instructions:

1. Heat skillet on medium heat, softening 2 tablespoons of butter in a pan.
2. Fry the scallops for 6 minutes on one side, turn over, and cook for an extra 2 minutes.
3. While scallops are cooking, add two tablespoons of butter to 2/3 cup of cream. Heat to the point of boiling and then stew until scallops are finished.

4. Place scallops on a plate and pours cream sauce on top.

Soup and Broth Recipes Carnivores

Bone Broth

Ingredients:

- 3 pounds chicken, turkey, pork, meat, lamb, or fish bones with connective tissue
- 1/2 teaspoon peppercorns
- Tablespoon of vinegar
- Teaspoon of salt
- Water

Instructions:

1. Place the bones in a huge soup pan.
2. Fill with water until the bones are completely covered. Include peppercorns, vinegar, and salt.
3. Bring to a boil.
4. Reduce heat to a low stew. Ensure the fluid is as yet foaming.

5. Cover with the top marginally slightly open.
6. Cook for 24-48 hours.
7. 7. Pour through a strain to expel bones.
8. 8. Enjoy.

Steak Soup

Ingredients:

- Salt and pepper
- Water
- at least 1 steak bones
- Cubed or sliced steak
- 1 tablespoon of vinegar

Instructions:

1. Add ingredients to a soup pot. Include enough water to cover meat and bones—season to taste.
2. Bring to a boil.
3. Reduce heat and stew for 2-4 hours.
4. Remove bones.

Carnivore Lamb Stew

(Can substitute hamburger or chicken)

Ingredients:

- 4 cups of hamburger or bone stock
- One pound each of bone-in lamb shoulder and lamb shank
- ¼ cup of water

Instructions:

1. Season lamb with pepper, salt, and add to slow cooker.
2. Pour in soup and cook on low for 4-6 hours.
3. Remove lamb and shred, discarding bones.
4. Return lamb and fat to your cooker.
5. Add water and blend—Cook for an extra 30 minutes.

Oven-Baked Pork Ribs

Complete Prep and Cooking Time: 190 Minutes Yields: 3 Servings Nutrition Facts: Calories: 440 Protein: 25 g Net Carbs: 2 g Fat: 36 g

Ingredients:

- One rack of child back ribs (one pound)
- One tsp. garlic powder
- One tsp. chili powder
- One tsp. onion powder
- Half-tsp. cayenne pepper
- One tsp. smoked paprika
- One tsp. salt
- Parchment paper
- Baking plate

Instructions:

1. Prepare your heating plate with the parchment paper while setting your oven to preheat at 275°F.
2. Mix your flavoring up in a bowl and set aside.
3. Remove the film from your ribs on the backside and dry them off.
4. Rub the flavoring blend into the ribs until the two sides are entirely covered.
5. Put the ribs on your rack and let them cook in your preheated oven for 3 hours.

Pork ribs are a delicious choice for supper and give left-overs that continue giving. This is a decent recipe to toss in the oven while you exercise or complete some work, because of the long cook time. You can marinate the ribs medium-term in their spices before cooking to get a significantly more profound flavor.

Pulled Chicken

All out Prep and Cooking Time: 6-7 Hours Yields: 4 Servings Nutrition Facts: Calories: 510 Protein: 55 g Net Carbs: 2 g Fat: 30 g

Ingredients:

- Six boneless and skinless chicken thighs
- One-third cup of salted butter
- One-quarter cup red wine vinegar
- One-quarter cup natural chicken stock
- Two tbsp. yellow mustard
- Two tbsp. spiced mustard
- One tbsp. cumin
- One tbsp. chili powder
- Two tbsp. water

- One tsp. cayenne pepper
- One stick of butter
- Crockpot/slow cooker
- One estimating cup

Instructions:

1. Combine your chicken stock, red wine vinegar, mustard, water, chili powder, cumin, and cayenne pepper into an estimating cup.
2. Throw either new or solidified chicken thighs into the crockpot/slow cooker.
3. Pour your flavoring blend on top.
4. If you will be going out, including 33% of a cup of butter and set the crockpot to low heat for seven hours, this is to guarantee nothing burns, but you, despite everything get a new meal when you are home.

Conclusion

Appreciation goes to you for creating time to read this book. We trust that this book has been educational and enlightening and has given you enough data to assist you with deciding if some type of carnivore diet is for you. While numerous hardcore practitioners of the diet restrict themselves to steak, salt, and water, it is conceivable to appreciate a shifted diet of animal products and spices while as yet being on a carnivore diet. By strictly restricting your carbs and admission of plant-based products, you should get yourself increasingly ready to reach your health, wellness, and weight loss objectives. Utilize the recipes in the keep going chapter for thoughts on the best way to make the diet increasingly agreeable. Good luck with your progress!

Made in the USA
Monee, IL
22 October 2020

45816935R00125